GEORGE CRUIKSHANK
His Life and London

GEORGE CRUIKSHANK
His Life and London

Michael Wynn Jones

M

Wynn Jones, Michael
    George Cruikshank.
    1. Cruikshank, George   2. Cartoonists—England
    —Biography
    741'.092'4   NC242.C7

    ISBN 0-333-22006-4

First published 1978 by
MACMILLAN LONDON LIMITED
4 Little Essex Street, London, WC2R 3LF
and Basingstoke
Associated Companies in Delhi, Dublin,
Hong Kong, Johannesburg, Lagos, Melbourne,
New York, Singapore and Tokyo

Filmset and printed in Great Britain by
BAS Printers Limited
Over Wallop, Hampshire

Contents

Illustrations

Preface

In February 1978 it will be one hundred years since the death of one of Britain's greatest illustrators. Yet in all that time only one significant account of his life has been published, and that four years after his death. For a number of reasons Blanchard Jerrold's *Life of George Cruikshank* is, for all its obvious virtues, a rather unsatisfactory record (in common with other memoirs and essays published just after the artist's death). Most of those writers knew Cruikshank only as a dedicated temperance advocate, and had but a hazy knowledge of most of his active career. Jerrold himself had access to few letters or personal drafts and relied heavily on hearsay accounts. His verdict on Cruikshank's claims to have 'originated' several novels, for instance, was manifestly prejudiced by his own loyalty to others still living – and it is Jerrold's uncontested verdict that, until recently, has coloured all subsequent judgements.

Jerrold, and possibly other would-be biographers, were certainly constrained at the time by Eliza Cruikshank, George's second wife, who insisted that she had possession of George's 'autobiography' which in due course would be edited and published. In the event this autobiography turned out to be virtually non-existent; several sketches and a few scanty pages of notes were all it comprised. Nevertheless, the promise – or the threat – of it remained until Mrs Cruikshank's death in 1890. By then all those whose childhoods had been filled with Cruikshank's images were old men themselves, and George was remembered only by collectors or the few who penetrated into that little corner of the old Westminster Aquarium where his permanent exhibition was housed. In 1902, even that was dispersed.

In fact George Cruikshank, even before his death, had outlived his popularity: the social conditions that had inspired his satire and humour were growing remote. His first published work had appeared the year after Trafalgar, over seventy years before. No one has accurately estimated the sum total of his output, but the suggested figure of 15,000 separate etchings, sketches, watercolours and oil-paintings is probably no understatement. Together they add up to a unique record of three distinct ages – the Regency, the Reform and the mid-Victorian eras. They document the changing patterns of society high and low, of popular fiction and – above all – of London itself. Few artists have observed a city with such affection as he did, and surely none has recorded its life over three generations in such detail and with such unfailing good humour.

Until recently Cruikshank's work as a whole has been sadly neglected in Britain. (Strangely, he has been more popular in the United States, where several of the great collections have been preserved and are still being added to.) Fortunately there are signs that once again his genius is being more widely appreciated, as art historians and literary scholars begin to quarry the great deposits of his work. This present book owes much to the fruits of their labours over the past five years. It is not intended to be a critical analysis of Cruikshank's art, but rather a record of his life in London in the light of the new evidence which has recently surfaced. So intimately was he involved with his surroundings, with the events of the day and the prevailing conditions of society, that it is impossible to divorce his work from them, and it is on this basis that the tiny fraction of his output illustrated here has been chosen.

The adjective most commonly applied to George Cruikshank by his friends was 'inimitable', expressing both a respect for his art and an appreciation of his colourful character. His art remains but his character is more elusive: this book is an attempt to find out what his contemporaries meant by the word, which in an age of colourful characters was not one to be used lightly.

MICHAEL WYNN JONES

GEORGE CRUIKSHANK
His Life and London

1 'Cradled in Caricature'
(1792-1811)

At ten o'clock on Thursday, 9 January 1806 there assembled at Hyde Park Corner a funeral procession, the like of which London had never before witnessed for a commoner. Since early morning the muffled drums had echoed round the city, summoning soldiers and spectators alike to witness the last rites of Lord Nelson, just eleven weeks after he had fallen on the very brink of victory at Trafalgar. Now the vast cortège was ready to move off, led by the band of the Old Buffs playing 'Rule Britannia' and the 92nd and 79th Regiments proudly bearing the standards that had been shot to pieces in the Egyptian campaign. Then followed more regiments, their bands and trumpets, the Royal Artillery with its cavalcade of field-pieces, the grenadiers, then the seamen and marines of H.M.S. *Victory*, then marshals and heralds, divines and city deputations, court officials and personal attendants. In the distance Nelson's own banner as Knight of the Bath heralded the passage of the highest in the land, more than one hundred mourning coaches laden with earls, marquesses, royal dukes – and, unmistakably, the ripening bulk of the Prince of Wales himself. Another great banner passed, with carriages bearing the arms and crests of the deceased: ten admirals followed and then, at last, the funeral-car, an ornate and splendid carved replica of *Victory*, escutcheoned and canopied and inscribed with the list of his glorious triumphs. There upon its quarter-deck lay the coffin and a single English Jack fluttering at half-mast. Finally, and poignantly, Nelson's own coach closed the procession, empty, with its blinds drawn up.

Slowly the host advanced, through St James's Park and up the Strand. At Temple Bar there was a pause as the Lord Mayor and Corporation of London greeted the procession and formally admitted it to their City. Every window in Fleet Street, festooned with crêpe, was crammed with faces; every inch of pavement and alleyway teemed with silent spectators, straining to glimpse this masterpiece of pomp and pageant. Somewhere – if we could see him in the throng – was a thirteen-year-old boy, his gaze fixed on that heroic funeral-car, scrutinising each inscription, each sable plume and cypress wreath. Perhaps he had stationed himself at the corner of the street where he lived, where, propped up on his father's shoulders, he had seen other such processions pass on their way to St Paul's – though nothing like this one. More likely he had taken his stand before dawn at the top of Ludgate Hill, for here the funeral-car would stop outside the western gate of the cathedral, while the pallbearers removed the coffin. That would give him more time for his sketches.

If anyone gave a second glance to the young lad sketching at the kerbside, they would surely have been struck at once by the confidence of his line and the precision of his detail. And perhaps, when the crowds thinned out, they might have seen him threading his way back to Dorset Street with his clutch of papers, to climb up to his father's studio and work out his finished drawing. Two months later, even (to stretch the web of coincidence still further), they might have opened their magazine, dimly recalled those bold outlines of the funeral-car and the boy sketching by St Paul's, and curiously noted the rough-and-ready signature at the bottom: Cruikshank.

When thirteen-year-old George, the younger son of Isaac Cruikshank, published his sketch of Nelson's funeral-car, Britain stood virtually alone in Europe against the indomitable advance of the new French Empire. The year that he was born, 1792, however – indeed the very same week in September – France had been on the edge of disintegration, a self-proclaimed republic torn between feuding Jacobins and Girondins, its borders invaded by both Prussia and Austria. Yet within months the revolutionaries of Paris had turned on their enemies and thrown down the challenge to every monarchy in Europe. From then on, and for the whole of George's childhood (with one uneasy interlude of fourteen months) Britain was at war with France, with her subversive revolutionary ideas within and her Grand Army abroad. The momentous events of the turn of the century inevitably coloured George's upbringing, for his father was by then one of London's foremost political cartoonists: each week the fortunes of war were discussed and the bulletins from overseas analysed – to be translated into a regular supply of satires that issued from the Cruikshank household to print-sellers all over town. By the time he was twelve, George was already contributing to his father's political plates and French parodies, and acquiring that hatred of the French which remained with him for the rest of his life.

Isaac Cruikshank was a Scottish exile. At one time his father had been a customs official in Leith, before the family drifted into hard times – perhaps, as George liked to boast, because of their involvement at Culloden, or perhaps not. At all events, tradition has it that he moved into Edinburgh to scrape a living as an artist and it was there, in the parish of Canongate, that Isaac was born on 5 October 1764 (the son of 'Andrew Crookshanks').* Following in the same profession Isaac, too, found occupation scarce in the Scottish capital and after his father died, while he was still in

2

his teens, he took the familiar path to London (as Allan Ramsay had done before him and David Wilkie was to do after him), armed only with a certain talent with watercolours and the etching-needle.

He arrived in London in or about 1783. It was an opportune moment for a destitute engraver to arrive. The print-shops which had blossomed in the first half of the eighteenth century and had prospered exceedingly during the late American war were now an established part of the social scene in the capital, fashionable salons where politically minded gentlemen could absorb a jaundiced view of affairs at their leisure, and hostesses could purchase the latest item of scandal for their next dinner-party. Artists like Richard Dighton and James Sayers, and more particularly James Gillray and Thomas Rowlandson, were transforming the coarse drolleries of their anonymous predecessors into elegant and cutting works of art. The demand for topical prints was insatiable and both the politics and the morals of the day, equally uninhibited, offered a constant source of new material. For anyone with a ready wit the opportunities were there, and Isaac had soon graduated from producing cheap chapbooks and lottery-tickets, the staple fare of jobbing engravers, to being a regular supplier of the West End print-sellers. By the early 1790s he was acknowledged as a leading caricaturist – more Pittite than Radical (though typically willing to lend his pencil to any party if necessary), unsophisticated in technique and characterisation but humorous and incisive.

By this time he had met and married Mary MacNaughton, like himself an expatriate Scot. Her parents in Perth had both died while she was a child and she had been brought up under the wing of the Countess of Orkney – who seems to have had superior social ambitions for her, since any hints of the wedding to a mere artist had to be concealed from her. The couple settled in Bloomsbury, where their first son, Robert, was born on 27 September 1789. George followed three years later, to the day. It was soon clear that Mary Cruikshank had brought south with her all the traditional virtues of her homeland; she was independent and self-willed, and given over at times to flashes of Highland temper. Thrifty and frugal, she was a devout member of the congregation of the Scottish Church in Drury Lane. She knew Jerusalem, she said, as well as she knew Camden Town. Above all, she was an excellent mother, as well she might be with Isaac for a husband. By temperament a docile and reflective fellow, and indulgent father – Mary, he sometimes complained, was needlessly strict with her children – he would nevertheless decline into prolonged bouts of drinking, not least when his wife had invited some clergyman round for the evening, and no words of hers could keep him out of the Ben Jonson tavern when he had a mind to. But with Mary's economies and his own recognition as an artist – by 1792 Isaac had become an

3

I

occasional exhibitor at the Royal Academy – they were able in due course to leave Bloomsbury (not then the fashionable quarter it was to become) and set up a more spacious establishment near Fleet Street.

George was three when they moved to the house in Dorset Street, one of a small labyrinth of streets running down to the Thames to the south of Fleet Street, and it was to be his home for the next twenty-five years. When he was in his seventies he drew a picture of 117 Dorset Street, from memory: it depicts a well-proportioned early eighteenth-century terraced house, four-storied and built characteristically around an alleyway leading to the rear. The windows are neatly draped, and an elegant iron lamp illuminates the entrance to the passage. The impression is distinctly one of sober, comfortable, middle-class well-being and, more than anything, of spaciousness. Doubtless that is what George wished to convey, but we do know it was a large dwelling since it accommodated Isaac's studio and workrooms on the top floor and living quarters for the family and household, which included a children's nurse, and still left room for Mrs Cruikshank to take in lodgers.

On the right-hand chimney-stack in George's drawing an observant viewer will notice a young boy clinging on to the brickwork for dear life, some forty feet above the street. It is George himself, and he is stuck. In a stomach-churning attempt to

2

4

negotiate the narrow roof-ledge, his jacket has caught on an errant nail: he can neither move nor dare to release his hold on the chimney-stack to disentangle himself. With the clarity with which old men can often recollect trifling incidents of their youth, George meticulously etched each detail of this incident in a close-up version 'for posterity' as he put it. He claimed he had 'always looked upon any form of autobiography as a vanity', which was why – in spite of the urgings of his friends – he failed ever to pen more than a few consecutive sentences of reminiscences. However, he did complete a short series of sketches, cameos of his childhood, which are entirely autobiographical: George's concept of vanity never extended to self-portraiture, though these sketches for 'A Handbook for Posterity' were not published until 1895,* and then only in a small limited edition for private circulation under the title *Drawings by George Cruikshank*.

The charm of these drawings (they make no pretence to be works of art) lies in their ingenuousness. Narrated rather than drawn, these events of his youth, of which the chimney-stack episode was one, might seem commonplace, and yet they are precisely the kind of keepsakes of childhood that we all retain. A writer might reject them – but not an artist. We see in the first frame of George's peep-show a family group, up in Hampstead: little Robert, George in his nurse's arms, and their mother feeding some chickens. What made this a memorable occasion is what happened next (in the second frame). Suddenly the fence on which Mrs Cruikshank is leaning gives way, and she is toppling in all her finery into a duckpond. The day is saved, as it happens, by a dairyman who has seen the accident and fishes her out – but the sequel was not so amusing. Mother was ill for weeks afterwards, and prematurely gave birth to her youngest child, Eliza, who was herself never very strong.

George's father appears in the next tableau, entitled 'A Threat'. The lad, we must take it, has misbehaved and is consequently being dangled out of a window by his father: he swears repentance, begs for mercy and promises to be a good boy for ever. But Isaac looks anything but wrathful and the likelihood of the 'threat' being carried out, as they both know, is utterly remote. Anyway, all is forgiven in the next scene which probably dates from summer 1801. Young George sits on his father's shoulders, in a crowd at the corner of Dorset Street and Fleet Street: a procession passes, King George III in his state coach is riding to St Paul's to give thanks for his deliverance – once again – from one of his bouts of insanity. Nor was this George's only close-up of His Majesty. The scene changes to the strip of wasteland outside the royal mews (what is now Trafalgar Square), where the boy has been happily flying his kite. Without ceremony a grand carriage drives by, whose occupant George recognises immediately as the King. He lets go of his kite and, jumping up and down, waves furiously. Sad to say, the King has not noticed the lad for, had he done so, the affable old gentleman would surely have waved back.

There are other fleeting boyhood recollections: here is George learning to prime a tinderbox – an everyday chore that later generations knew nothing of – and here being taken with Robert by his mother to school at the Scottish Church, and in another vignette a near-disaster. The boys and their father have been making homemade fireworks for Guy Fawkes' night in the cellar, but something has gone wrong. The room is erupting around them and the startled chemists have been blown off their feet.

A noticeable omission from George's panorama of his youth (there are further episodes recalled, which we shall encounter in due course) is any memory of his schooldays. Both he and his brother were briefly sent to a school in Edgware to acquire the rudiments of an elementary education, but the family resources could not indulge them more than that – a fact which George felt keenly in later life. The brothers were thrown early upon their own initiative to study, as Frederic Stephens lyrically put it, 'in the college of colleges . . . and to take the highest of all degrees'.* Robert elected to go to sea, inspired by the exotic stories of the explorer Mungo Park who for a time, between his first and his second, fatal voyage to West Africa, was one of Mrs Cruikshank's lodgers in Dorset Street. When he was fourteen Robert joined the East India Company as a midshipman, and was away from home for three years. For a few terrible months in 1805 he was feared drowned: on a return journey to England he had been put in command of a landing party going ashore on St Helena. A sudden squall blew up and his ship sailed off, giving him up for lost, somewhat prematurely since he managed to survive on the island until rescued by a passing whaler. On that homeward trip, he recalled, they heard news of the great victory at Trafalgar from an outward-bound vessel. There was also a family tradition that Robert had inscribed a cartoon of Napoleon on the wall of the shed where he had passed his shipwrecked days – which George commemorated in another of his 'posterity' sketches, showing the fallen Emperor coming across the cartoon ten years later in his days of exile on the same island!

George, too, was powerfully drawn to the sea and ships, but three years younger than his brother the nearest he got to a life on the ocean waves was a voyage, with his aunt and mother, from London Bridge to Margate in a sailing vessel then known as a 'hoy',* and frequent excursions down to his favourite wharf below the Adelphi. Here from the age of seven to ten, among the seamen and coal-heavers, beer-swilling and fist fights, he pencilled some of his very first sketches of life – which seventy years later formed the earliest exhibits at the great Cruikshank collection at the Westminster Aquarium. The fascination of the sea never deserted him – at least in its land-locked form, in the tales and shanties of weather-beaten sea-dogs on the river front – but his nautical ambitions obviously palled after Robert's experience, and evaporated after a narrow escape from the press-gang that came preying for bodies to fill their man-of-war. (H. S. Ashbee, to whom Cruikshank recounted the press-gang incident,* suggested it might have changed his whole career and deprived the world of a great fund of amusement. To which George replied 'with a simplicity that was one of the great charms of his conversation, "Well, I should have done my duty and become an admiral."')

His youthful relish for the military life, on the other hand, matured into something like zeal later on. His father, like many an able-bodied man during the frequent Napoleonic invasion scares, was a member of a local volunteer force, in his case the Loyal St Giles's and St George's Bloomsbury Volunteers. These part-timers took their duties very seriously, being roused by the bugle-horn at five in the morning and drilling from six until eight and training with their muskets in the evening. George would watch his father's regiment with a mixture of pride and awe, as it wheeled out of the courtyard of the old British Museum to march to Hyde Park for inspection, and wholeheartedly joined his elder brother when he took it upon himself to found his own children's 'regiment' (and appoint himself colonel). As he recounts:*

> We had our drum and fife, our 'colours' presented by our mammas and sisters, who also assisted in making our accoutrements. We also procured small 'gun-stocks' into which we fixed mopsticks for barrels, kindly polished by Betty with a tinge of blacklead, to make 'em look like *real* barrels. The boys watched their fathers drill; and 'as the old cock crows the young one learns', so we children followed in the steps of our papas, and we were ready for inspection quite as soon as our elders, and could march in good order to have *our* 'field-day' from Bloomsbury Church to the fields where Russell and Tavistock Squares now stand.

All this juvenile drilling, George maintained, would have enabled him to 'fall into the ranks of an infantry regiment at a moment's notice', but it was not to be: his thirst for military glory had to be quenched by nothing more heady than a couple of spells in adult volunteer corps. For the truth of the matter was that George's vocation was unmistakable long before the time came to choose a career: he was born to the sound of copper plates being hammered out, and with the smell of aquafortis in his nostrils. His father's studio, around which all the comings and goings of the household revolved, very early became the centre of his curiosity and then of his enthusiasm. To use his own phrase, he was 'cradled in caricature', he inherited from his father not just the journeyman's skill of engraving but an oblique vision of the world, which was the foundation for George's development as a caricaturist.

We can only imagine what Isaac's studio must have been like: its rows of jars, varnish and acids and Brunswick black, its sheets of burnished copper reflecting like mirrors, its racks of etching-needles, gravers and scrapers. We must imagine, too, George's expeditions to the top of the house to watch his father at work, chiselling out his designs in box-wood or biting out his plates with bubbling acid. But the artist himself tells us that he was only 'a mere boy when my dear father kindly allowed me to *play* at etching on some of his copper plates'.* At first it was just 'little bits of shadows or little figures in the background' with which he was entrusted, but as George's own facility at drawing improved he was allowed to graduate to outlines and even whole compositions, with his father finishing off the more difficult anatomical features, the hands and the faces. One example of such a collaboration between father and son seems to be *Facing the Enemy*, probably published in 1803, the year in which the Peace of Amiens broke down and Britain found herself once more at war with France. In this print an alarmingly robust guardsman confronts an ill-fed and forlorn Frenchman and sportingly debates whether 'to give the fellow a meal before I fight him'. Their faces look to be by Isaac, but much of the rest of the very creditable design proclaims eleven-year-old George to have acquired already the intuitive touch of the engraver.

George's progress must have impressed several of the print-sellers who dropped into Dorset Street from time to time; before he was a year older George was being given commissions of his own, to produce children's lottery prints. The State lottery in those days was still a popular form of gambling, and a colourful one, the lottery-agents organising grand displays and processions to advertise their tickets. A number of printers capitalised very profitably on this national mania by producing lottery 'puffs' as a game for children – sheets of small, simple designs that would be cut up and inserted between the leaves of books as 'prizes' for children who held the lucky numbers. By their very nature these designs were particularly ephemeral, but several of George's efforts have survived, including one of his very first, for W. Belch of Newington Butts. Its sixteen separate designs depict different trades and professions, and in the left-hand corner is a portrait of young George himself delivering his finished copperplate – this apparently at the request of Mr Belch whose name appears over the bookshop.* Nevertheless, it created a precedent for the artist to sneak himself into his own drawings, which he was still doing sixty years later.

In between helping his father more drawings followed, some 'raceing' scenes and landscape views all of which found publishers and, as we have seen, his sketch of Nelson's hearse. By the time brother Robert returned from his nautical adventures he found George already established on a career and he resolved to join the family firm, as it were, himself. Robert proved to be a meticulous draughtsman with a special aptitude for portraits, though he was often obliged to seek George's help in transferring his drawings to wood or copper. The results of all this collusion between father and sons and brothers (with, at the same time, we are told, Mrs Cruikshank quietly colouring in finished prints) led 'to a considerable amount of confusion' George later told his cataloguer,* 'so that dealers or print-sellers and collectors have been puzzled to decide which were the productions of the I.Ck. the I.R.Ck. [his brother then being known as Isaac Robert] and the G.Ck.; and this will not create much surprise when I tell you that I have myself, in some cases, had a difficulty in deciding in respect to early handwork, done some sixty odd years back . . .'.

George's apprenticeship with his father was equipping him well enough with the techniques of the etcher's trade, but as an artist he felt himself handicapped by the lack of any formal training. Yet he clearly had a natural gift for composition that promised to outstrip his father's, and was remarkable for his age. When he was twelve, on his own initiative, he submitted some drawings to Henry Fuseli, who was then Keeper of the Royal Academy and professor of painting, in the hope of winning admission to the Academy schools. Fuseli's reply to the young Cruikshank was that he would have to 'fight for a place' – though whether this ambiguous advice referred to a seat at his own lectures on art which were invariably packed, or to a place at the schools, remains in doubt. At all events there is no record of any formal application from George: perhaps he was disappointed by the professor's equivocal reaction to his work, or perhaps the routine of academic training did not really appeal to him (almost fifty years later he *did* enter the Royal Academy as a student, only to tire very quickly of sketching classical statuary).

The artist himself offers us a singular reason for any short-comings we may detect in his boyish designs. He begs '. . . some excuse must be made for the inferiority of the earlier productions of his pencil – for although the son of an artist of considerable talent as a watercolour draughtsman and an etcher contemporary with Gillray (and some of his etching may be placed as equal to the works of that great artist), yet his son, George Cruikshank, did not wish, it appears, to be an artist, but an actor. . . .'* And indeed here – like the martial aspirations of his childhood – is revealed another strand of frustrated ambition, which was to thread itself through the rest of his life.

George's devotion to the theatre, and to Drury Lane in particular, had long been apparent. Theatrical portraits were one of his father's stocks-in-trade and one of his regular publishers was a man by the name of Roach, who happened to live in Vinegar Yard near Drury Lane. To his house George and Robert were doubtless regularly dispatched with the completed portraits, and it was there the brothers made the acquaintance of Edmund Kean (then a lad of Robert's age, being brought up by a small-part actress with the Drury Lane company). Even then Kean was displaying those precocious talents that, some fifteen years later, were to make him the undisputed prince of tragedy on the London stage, and the young Cruikshanks were roped into impromptu performances to play supporting parts to Kean's starring roles. Much later, Robert was to commemorate one of their amateur theatricals in Roach's kitchen in a watercolour sketch: a performance of Bluebeard with the kitchen copper doing duty as the tyrant's castle.

Kean in his most celebrated roles – Shylock, Richard III, Hamlet – was to become a favourite subject for both artists, and he remained their drinking-companion even while he was drinking himself to a slow death. But the theatrical giant of George's youth – after the statuesque manner of his day – was John Kemble, tragedian and manager of the Covent Garden theatre. Kemble was, in fact, the not over-flattered subject of George's earliest attempt at a serial print, *The Stroller's Progress* (1809), depicting the actor's career from failed priest to successful actor to bankruptcy. Kemble's misfortune was to see his Covent Garden theatre burned to the ground in 1808 (the same year, curiously, as Drury Lane was also destroyed by fire). Hardly was the rubble of the old building cool – so we observe from another of his 'posterity' sketches – than George was round there with his sketch-pad to record this momentous disaster for a magazine. Alas, as he clambered through the burnt-out skeleton he was mistaken by a militiaman presumably for a looter, apprehended with the point of a bayonet under his collar, and removed from the scene (or so Charles Hancock's interpretation of this particular episode ran, based, he said, on the evidence of his own conversations with George).*

By the following year a new and magnificent Covent Garden, resplendent with Doric portico, had risen out of the ashes. Unfortunately, such was the expensive taste with which the new theatre had been decorated and equipped that Kemble was obliged to raise the prices of pits and boxes. The first-nighters on 18 September 1809 were so incensed by this that they staged a riot, as had happened several times in the previous century, forcing the performance of *Macbeth* starring Kemble and his sister, Mrs Siddons, to be abandoned. These demonstrations, dubbed 'the Old Price riots', continued for three months until Kemble was forced to submit and restore the old prices. George's sympathies were with the audience – almost certainly he was one of the rioters, to judge from the broadsides of satire that were fired at the head of poor Kemble from Dorset Street: between them George and his father executed at least fourteen O.P. propaganda prints that October and November. So it was not entirely surprising, then, that when George began seriously to contemplate a career in the theatre a little later on, it was not to Mr Kemble that he applied but to the rival establishment up the road, Drury Lane. A few modest successes in local juvenile plays may have kindled adolescent yearnings after stardom,* but they evidently weren't so all-consuming that he was prepared to endure the customary apprenticeship – then as now, a few seasons in the provinces with an itinerant company. George's shortcut to fame and fortune – with the help of some acquaintances already in the company – was to apply for a job as scene-painter to the manager of the newly opened Drury Lane theatre, James Grand Raymond. (Raymond – though in a much kindlier guise than Kemble – also appeared in several of Cruikshank's plates, mainly to do with an abortive competition for a Prologue to be spoken at the re-opening of the theatre. The entries were so bad that Byron was eventually prevailed upon to compose it.) One drop-scene he is known to have painted, a caricature of a well-known gourmandising alderman, was greeted with general approval,* but for whatever reason he failed thereafter to follow his inclinations. Acting, like soldiering, became a preoccupation of his leisure; mercifully, one suspects – for however entertaining his extrovert and improvised 'performances' after dinner were, he was never really reconciled to the studied disciplines of even the amateur stage.

Maybe common sense prevailed: to have forsaken a craft that was already a significant source of income for the hazardous lure of the greasepaint must have struck his family as sheer perversity. Mrs Cruikshank had no illusions. 'Without their pencils in their hands,' she remarked of both her sons, 'they are a couple of boobies'. Besides, George had by now come to the attention of the more fashionable print-sellers – Fores' of Piccadilly, Rudolph Ackermann in the Strand, Thomas Tegg of Cheapside – as an up-and-coming satirist in his own right. Creative talent was not so thick on the ground, after all, since the premature death of Robert Newton or since Gillray had signed exclusively for Humphrey's, and Rowlandson grown fitful in his political inspiration. Just after his fifteenth birthday, in 1807, George had produced for a small publisher just off the Strand his first political plate, all his own work and proudly signed 'G. Cruikshank'. Entitled *Cobbett at Court*, it portrayed the troublesome radical turning up at St James's with an address to the King under his arm: a modest effort, but already displaying some of those expressive Cruikshankian touches soon to become familiar in print-sellers' windows.

The following year another solo production by George, *The Rogue's March from Madrid to Paris*, was accepted by Ackermann. This topical print, ridiculing the flight of Napoleon's puppet, Joseph Buonaparte, from Spain at the first murmurings of national revolt, was signed (lest there be any doubt) 'George Cruikshank Junr.' – a designation he subsequently abandoned. And over the next eighteen months several more trifles under George's name appeared in publishers' portfolios, including that of Fores: the fact there were not more may be put down to the pressure under which Isaac's studio must have been working at that time – there are at least twenty prints on the splendid scandal of Mrs Clarke in 1809 alone,* not to mention flurries of satires on Napoleon, the war in Spain, the riots at Covent Garden, the duel between Castlereagh and Canning, General Whitelocke's pusillanimous withdrawal from Buenos Aires, and kindred subjects. In some of these George's hand appears to predominate, but where a plate carries a signature it is left deliberately ambiguous, simply 'Cruikshank'.

Then, in 1810, this cascade of prints dwindled, quite suddenly, to a mere eighteen. In the absence of any reports of illness we might reasonably assume Isaac's intemperance had finally caught up with him: certainly George's recollections of coming downstairs in the mornings, and having to step over the recumbent bodies of his father's drinking-companions sleeping it off, were quite specific. And if the sketch 'A Dinner in a Tavern' in Isaac's hand is a portrait of the family – as the autograph notations in the margin suggest – a taste for liquor (and ladies) had been bequeathed to his sons even before his death. One figure (Robert) has a woman on his knees, another is obscured by a mug of ale, yet another has dozed off. Isaac himself, a whisky drinker, was popularly believed to have died drinking – as a result of a bet that he could down more whiskies than his rival and still stay on his feet. He won the bet, George told a friend long afterwards, but it brought on a fatal illness: and if his last published print (6 September 1810) is any guide – for no record of his burial has survived – he probably did not live to see his younger son's eighteenth birthday.

2 Personalities
(1811-1815)

'Knight's in Sweeting's Alley, Fairburn's in a court off Ludgate Hill, Hone's in Fleet Street – bright enchanted palaces which George Cruikshank used to people with grinning, fantastical imps and merry, harmless sprites – where are they?' lamented William Thackeray in the soberer days of 1840. 'How we used to stray miles out of the way on holidays, in order to ponder for an hour before that delightful window in Sweeting's Alley! in walks through Fleet Street to vanish abruptly down Fairburn's passage, and there make one at his charming "gratis" exhibition. There used to be a crowd round the window in those days of grinning good-natured mechanics, who spelt the songs, and spoke them out for the benefit of the company, and who received the points of humour with a general sympathising roar . . . .'*

Thackeray was just old enough to remember the print-shops in the days of their prosperity, before they were extinguished like burnt-out stars or else declined into purveyors of polite and genteel humour; in the days when Prinny might still have driven down St James's past crowds outside Humphrey's gloating over the latest caricature of his newest mistress, or Wellington taken a turn down Piccadilly to be greeted by his own grotesquely angular features in Fores' window. Between the rulers and the ruled in Georgian England there were many unbridgeable gulfs, but in the print-shops these melted away if only for a moment; princes could become philanderers, prime ministers babbling old fools, and Parliament a garrulous motley of pensioners. The victims tolerated it even if they did not like it, thinking perhaps, and with good reason, that as long as an Englishman could laugh at authority he was less likely to assault it. For the best party of a century, while pamphleteers had been indicted for sedition and demagogues hauled off to gaol, the print-sellers had survived more or less unscathed – their excesses curbed more effectively by bribes than by bluster. Again, Thackeray mainly recalled George's 'fantastical imps' on display in the print-shops, but in the very year he was born (1811) the nineteen-year-old artist was launching himself on an independent career that promised to be anything but 'harmless'. The death of their father clearly involved the brothers in a reappraisal of their working arrangements: they decided to keep on the studio in Dorset Street, and with their mother and sister continuing their role as landladies to pay the household

13

expenses. From annotations on prints in George's hand it is clear the brothers went on working closely together for some time, though George later insisted there was no 'contract' between them. Robert did not begin producing prints on his own account until later in 1814, and seems rather to have appropriated the function of 'ideas-man' and designer.

For George, however, a new and promising market soon materialised. Johnston, the Cheapside print-seller for whom he had already produced a few plates, had a couple of years earlier followed Tegg's example in opening a 'Caricature Warehouse' offering prints at wholesale prices. Its success, like modern supermarkets, depended on a quick turnover and it was a voracious consumer of ideas (during the Clarke scandal he had promised, over-optimistically, a new plate on the subject every day). At the end of 1810 Johnston decided to bolster his operation by going into partnership with the Jones family (known to posterity only by their initials M. and W.N.), who were starting an illustrated satirical magazine called *The Scourge* or 'Monthly Expositor of Imposture and Folly'. The first issue appeared on 1 January 1811, and from the sixth number, in June, George became the magazine's resident caricaturist.

The magazine had a good pedigree: it took its name from a vehement weekly called *The Scourge* which had belaboured Lord North unrelentingly in 1780, but it was more of a direct descendant of Whig-ish journals of the late eighteenth century like the *Oxford* and *London Magazines* which had first used caricature with effect. More recently Samuel Tipper's *Satirist* (1808) had set new standards in political venom and social scurrility, though visually it was disappointing. *The Scourge*, on the other hand, made a big feature of George's plates, huge coloured folding broadsheets (which could also be sold as prints), crammed with personalities, innuendo, and bad taste. George's work for *The Scourge*, which occupied him on and off for five years, has been neglected largely because later prurient generations found them profoundly shocking – and the artist himself virtually disowned them. Compared with his more mature prints these satires are crudely-drawn and vulgar in spirit: but by the same token they are boldly confident, fearless and funny.

George's broadsides spare no one, from the newly founded yet senile Royal College of Surgeons to the ridiculous pantomime at Covent Garden where an elephant appeared on stage. Brewers who were profiteering on the sixpenny pint of porter; intrigues within the Antiquarian Society; the patrician decadence of the ostentatious Four-in-Hand Club (the Cavendish Square aristocracy who spent princes' ransoms on their horses); the 'visitation' of the aged Joanna Southcott who daily expected to give birth to the Messiah – all these came under the merciless scrutiny of *The Scourge*, along with more momentous issues like Lord Liverpool's government, the war with

Napoleon and the trade dispute with America. But the magazine's juiciest target was the Royal Circle, with its train of royal dukes and entourage of secret wives and brazen mistresses.

The threat of a Regency, which had loomed since the old king George III's first bout of insanity more than twenty years before, became a reality in February 1811. In place of the stubborn but undeniably moral old man the country now had to reconcile itself to his scandalous, spendthrift son. The image of Prinny that is stamped on history has been heavily coloured by the cartoonists, not least of them Cruikshank: flabby-jowled, tightly corseted, gross of appetite – for food, wine and women – incessantly in debt yet increasingly extravagant. The Regent's shortcomings needed little exaggeration, but even his more endearing aspects – his cultured tastes and social accomplishments – had never aroused much enthusiasm from the print-makers. George's plates for *The Scourge* were but the latest skirmishes in the campaign which Gillray and Rowlandson had first mounted in the 1780s.

Two plates from *The Scourge*, out of the dozens George drew of the Royal Family in the early years of the Regency, show what a precipitous path the artist was treading. In 'Princely Amusements' of March 1812 almost all the royal personages are pilloried for their adulterous behaviour. The Prince of Wales is the central figure flabbily capering in a reel (he fancied himself as a dancer) with his daughter Charlotte and Mrs Fitzherbert, his illegal wife: to his immense satisfaction his legitimate wife Princess Caroline, deserted and forlorn, makes her humiliating exit, while in the left-hand corner another of his elderly paramours, Lady Hertford, is manipulating her political puppets – as she was suspected of doing in real life. Three of the Royal Dukes, his brothers, are also introduced with their respective mistresses: the Duke of Clarence (later William IV) plays cards with the actress Mrs Jordan, by whom he had no less than eleven illegitimate children; their playing partners are the Duke of York and Mrs Carey (who has supplanted the devious Mrs Clarke). The Duke of Sussex lusts after the musical Mrs Billington, trampling all over the portrait of his deserted secret wife, Lady Augusta Murray.

The second plate of six months later is even more explicit in its sexual innuendoes. In 'The Coronation of the Empress of the Nairs' (the Nayars were a race that practised polyandry), Lady Hertford has ousted Mrs Fitzherbert in the Prince's affections, and here in all her buxom bath-time glory proclaims 'the freedom of the sex'. Whereupon all her female companions (including Princess Charlotte) take the initiative – a prospect which neither the Dukes of York and Cumberland (right) nor the detachment of grotesque grenadiers (left) find in the least unwelcome. The whole atmosphere and decor of the room, with its statues of Messalina and Aspasia and its memorials to the Prince's former mistresses, is reminiscent of a Roman orgy.

Neither of these examples is at all unrepresentative of the kind of vilification then being heaped on the Regent. Yet that same year (March 1812) Leigh Hunt, the editor of *The Examiner*, was put on trial for actually putting it into words: 'A violator of his word, a libertine over head and ears in debt and disgrace' was how he described him, 'a despiser of domestic ties, a man who has just closed half a century without one single claim on the gratitude of his country or the respect of posterity!' For that, Hunt was fined one thousand pounds and sentenced to two years in gaol. Even the shameless *Scourge* thought twice about writing specifically what was on its mind. In the same issue as George's 'Princely Amusements' it informed its readers of a frank piece of self-censorship:

> We had devoted the space that is now occupied by the present explanation [the editorial ran] to some just but not indecorous strictures on the conduct of our Princes, and the general character of their connections. After the impression had been printed off we submitted the article to the inspection of a legal gentleman, who informed us that whatever might be the truth of our remarks, their publication would subject us to the visitations of the Attorney-General. We have no desire to devote ourselves as martyrs to the liberty of the press, and we have therefore cancelled the offensive paragraph.*

Nevertheless, it did not occur to them for a moment to dispense with George's caricature as well.

And yet, in this reckless flirtation with the law, there do appear to have been limits – though how far George heeded them, or was even conscious of them, is open to doubt. In a much later number of *The Scourge* (August 1815), George contributed a plate entitled 'A Financial Survey of Cumberland', in celebration of the news that Parliament had refused to vote the Duke of Cumberland an increase in his Civil List income. The published caricature is distinctly unflattering to the Duke and the reputation of his new German wife, but it also contains a large area that has been obliterated with lamp-black. If it were not for the discovery of a single, uncoloured impression of the original plate* no-one would have known how close George might have come to languishing in one of His Majesty's prisons. For in its uncorrected state the caricature carries the figure of Cumberland's murdered valet, Sellis, his throat cut from ear to ear and looking in terror at a fearsome razor dripping with blood. Some years had passed since the discovery of the valet butchered in his bed, but rumours continued to circulate that it was Cumberland himself who had wielded the razor – that very year a journalist called Henry White had been sentenced to fifteen months' imprisonment for hinting no less. Clearly someone (probably Mr Jones the publisher) had decided after the prints had been run off that it was one thing to impugn royal morals, but quite another publicly to implicate a Royal Duke in murder.

Even granted that many of his subjects were suggested to him by others, George himself appears to have been remarkably insouciant about the possible consequences of some of his satires. In 1812 he produced a plate – not for *The Scourge* but, as he explained later in a handwritten note, privately for 'some libellous scoundrel' – on the scandalous situation at St Luke's Vestry, Chelsea, 'The Inside of a Newly Reformed Workhouse'. The parish vestries at that time fulfilled the functions of local councils, and were often chaotically and corruptly run. St Luke's in particular – as an enquiry in 1822 proved – was a hotbed of misappropriation and frauds such as are hinted at in this print: illegal payments for bastards, fiddling of the accounts and so on. Nevertheless, George's caricature gave rise to a libel action against Wood, a former Guardian of the Poor (who seems to have commissioned the print), by one Smith, the present incumbent of the office. George had taken the precaution of not signing the print and was not involved in the litigation (which proved fruitless); nevertheless he steered well clear of local politics after that.

At least there could be no question of libel with George's other select victim, Napoleon. From 1812 and the ill-fated retreat from Moscow, the Emperor's career accelerated towards the final disaster, attended by hoots of derision from the cartoonists as each new bulletin arrived from Europe. Not a month went by when George did not engrave some further instalment in the Emperor's downfall in one of the two new satirical magazines to have appeared on the scene, *Town Talk* (new series 1812–13) and *The Meteor* (1813–14), and culminating in his first full-length illustrated book *The Life of Napoleon* (1815) by 'Doctor Syntax', thirty plates spanning his career from military college to Elba. when Buonaparte's remains were removed to Paris some years later, George composed a tongue-in-cheek memorial to the Corsican upstart, acknowledging his debt to him:*

> I can scarcely remember the time when I did not take some patriotic pleasure in persecuting the great enemy of England. Had he been less than that, I should have felt compunction for my cruelties; having tracked him through snow and through fire, by flood and by field, insulting, degrading, and deriding him everywhere, and putting him to several humiliating deaths. All that time however . . . he went on playing at leap-frog with the sovereigns of Europe, so as to kick a crown off at every spring he made – together with many crowns and sovereigns into my coffers. Deep, most deep, in a personal view of matters, are my obligations to the Agitator.*

Since the turn of the century Napoleon's most unrelenting assailant had been James Gillray, his 'Little Boney' strutting across the map of Europe had become the Englishman's permanent image of his enemy. But now Gillray had lapsed into total incoherence, his uncontrolled hands wandering meaninglessly over the paper: his last completed plate was published by Hannah Humphrey in 1811, and his last four years were lived out in a state of mental and physical dereliction. The mantle of Gillray, it has often been said, fell on Cruikshank – and indeed in the progress of Little Boney it is almost as if Gillray had not ceased to engrave. George's diminutive tyrant is the same scrawny, dishevelled, wild-eyed fellow as Gillray's: his boots still don't fit, and his plumed hat still dwarfs him into insignificance.

Gillray's influence percolates into George's early political plates in other ways: his love of symbolic detail in the background, for instance, and his delight in catching the high-and-mighty in candid situations (stuffing their mouths with food, getting out of bed, slipping on the pavement). And echoes of Gillray's themes were to be found in Cruikshank's work for many years to come, for instance among others, *The Introduction of the Gout* (1818) an elaboration of Gillray's *The Gout* of 1799; and George's series of *Monstrosities* (1816–29) took its title and inspiration directly from his predecessor. George himself never disguised his admiration for (and debt to) Gillray. 'A great man, sir, a very great man,' he would say gravely, and on the artist's death in 1815 he acquired Gillray's work-table, as much an act of homage, one must suppose, as a symbol of continuity.

There was a popular tradition that Mrs Humphrey, recognising in young George the great man's heir apparent, engaged him to complete some of Gillray's unfinished plates. These have never been positively identified, and the notion may have been given currency by Cruikshank's association with Mrs Humphrey's nephew George after 1813, which produced some uncannily Gillrayesque designs. Several of these – from ideas by George Humphrey – were conceived as sequels to some of Gillray's most notable plates: thus 'Broken Gingerbread' (1814) is a reincarnation of Napoleon as the fast-talking Mayfair gingerbread-seller, only whereas Gillray had portrayed him in 1806 'baking' his puppet kings as fast as he can go, George has him here ludicrously trying to hawk his wares on the empty island of Elba. Likewise 'Boney's Meditations on the Island of St Helena' (1815) is a precise paraphrase of Gillray's 'Gloria Mundi' (1782) with Napoleon substituted for Charles James Fox and the Prince Regent for Shelburne. So effectively did Cruikshank recapture the style and spirit of the elder artist in these cartoons that it has even been suggested that, since Gillray was still alive when most of them were published, they were based on sketches penned by him during his rare lucid moments. But there is no contemporary witness to Gillray's tragic condition who suggests he was capable even of this.

By 1815, and with Rowlandson deeply involved in his continuing saga of the English Dance of Death, Cruikshank was recognised as the leading political caricaturist in London. Even the abrupt demise of *The Meteor* in 1814 and that of *The Scourge* in 1816 failed to affect his output: a survey of his work 1814–15 reveals that his prints were being published by over twenty of the thirty or so publishers known to have been in business in London in those years. The only important exceptions were Ackermann in the Strand, a connection that seems to have died with his father, and Holland who was himself at death's door. The prints paint a vivid portrait of the capital in the post-war years, its passions and preoccupations: the resurgence of 'frenchified' fashions in the form of towering Parisian bonnets, the quadrille, the mania for collecting Napoleonic souvenirs; the eternal controversy on what on earth to do with Lord Elgin's marbles, and the heated arguments over Herr Logier's revolutionary method of teaching the pianoforte; the curiously energetic craze for hobby-horses or velocipedes (soon banned in London streets), and the short-lived glory of George Wilson, the Blackheath 'pedestrian', whose attempt to walk a thousand miles in twenty days was thwarted by the local magistrates, who clapped him in gaol after seven hundred and fifty miles for causing a public disturbance; and in 'Introduction of Gas!!' (1815) the odours, explosions and general chaos occasioned by the laying of pipes for the new street-lamps – a heartfelt grumble no doubt from George, whose own street choked on 'the insufferable stench' from a nearby gas-works until the proprietor was prosecuted in November.*

With business so manifestly brisk, it is slightly curious to find George complaining of his lack of money. It was a refrain that recurred many times in his career, but at the period in which he engraved 'Hard Times' (the early part of 1814) there was no shortage of commissions. The print in question was prompted by the hardships in London that followed an exceptionally severe frost: among the gaggle of unemployed and down-at-heel figures in the picture there is George himself, threadbare and famished, and the satire is signed most pitifully 'Poor Shanks'. It might indeed be more of an ironical comment on his status than his income, especially as his fellow-artist is probably Benjamin West, whose portraits could command thousands of guineas. But there is also the evidence of one of his 'posterity' plates, which depicts a dilapidated garret, the windows and doors barricaded against duns. Inside George (clearly as a young man) prepares to defend himself against all-comers.

If there were impatient creditors and temporary pecuniary embarrassments then they were the result of George's own youthful and uninhibited pursuits. His mother's sharp tongue had no more success in keeping him or his brother out of the taverns than it had in curbing their father, and some taverns could be more of a drain on the pocket than others. The Castle Tavern in Holborn, where the two young men were 'regulars' for many years (George was still a familiar face at The Castle in the mid-1820s, judging from a scene in Clarke's *Every Night Book*), was the acknowledged headquarters of the prize-ring. The landlord was Tom Belcher, a noted pugilist of his day, and here each week the notorious Daffy Club met, the boozy assembly of all the great fistic heroes – Gentleman Jackson, Tom Cribb, Tom Spring, Hickman and Richmond – and their backers. An illustration to *The English Spy* includes the figure of Robert among this august fraternity, but in 'A Visit to the Fives Court' (in St Martin's Street, where sparring exhibitions were held) both brothers appear among the spectators, taking an informed interest in the proceedings, together with their journalist friend Pierce Egan. A great connoisseur of the Fancy, Egan had edited a couple of transient sporting publications, *Boxiana* (1812–13) and *The Boxing Mirror*, to which Robert and George had jointly contributed – amongst other plates – a graphic illustration of the second great contest between Tom Cribb and the black man Molineux (in which the latter fell with a shattered jaw).

Both George and his elder brother were keen amateur boxers and took lessons in the noble art at Gentleman Jackson's 'academy' in Bond Street – of which one memento, a broken nose, remained with George for the rest of his life. Any visitor to their workroom in Dorset Street, Blanchard Jerrold declared, was quite liable to be invited to a bout with the boxing-gloves amid all the bachelor clutter, which included 'an undergraduate cap upon a human skull with a pipe between the teeth, a sou'wester from Margate, boxing gloves, foils, masks, weapons of all kinds . . .'. George left a 'posterity' sketch of this same room: it has just the casual, sporty air that Jerrold describes. Foils and a fencing-mask are strewn about, sketches litter the table and floor, coats are dumped on the back of the door. George himself has drawn his chair up to the fireplace and is sketching characters on the painted lintel, already a kaleidoscope of doodles and unfinished drawings. (George's habit of sketching on the nearest thing to hand has left for us a mountain of scribbled-on envelopes, letter-heads, and fly-leaves. A screen in his studio at Myddleton Place was such a rich repository of doodles that it became a 'sight' for visitors to the house.) George thought nothing of rowing all the way up-river to Richmond, then rowing all the way back. He was a self-confessed fitness addict in spite of (or because of?) the punishment he could give a bottle or two, and even in his older, more temperate years took great delight in out-walking men half his age. He once listed as one of his favourite amusements 'athletic exercise', putting it second only to 'drilling',* a taste acquired (as we have seen) in early adolescence and confirmed when he was old enough by an exhilarating spell in a volunteer rifle company. Although his brother rose to the rank of sergeant in the 'Loyal North Britons', time deprived George of any promotion, but he was immensely proud of his spare-time regiment with its tight green trousers and tall plumage. Any man who dared, in customary fashion, to mock or jeer the Volunteers when George was around did so at his peril: one reckless fellow was collared and taught a lesson in the middle of Ludgate Hill. For 'drilling', he claimed without a trace of false modesty, he had a special aptitude, requiring only a brief acquaintance with the calls of the bugle to supplement what he already knew from the days of his 'Boys' Brigade' to become 'a tolerable rifleman one week after I had entered'. The highlight of his military service was a cherished memory – the Grand Review in Hyde Park after the Allies had entered Paris in 1814. 'Our regiment being commanded by a Royal Duke', he recalled, 'had the post of honour, next to the Royal troops; and as I had the honour of being present on that occasion I can assure my friends that we made a very respectable military appearance, and that the pop, pop, pop of our "feu de joie" was as regular as the pop, pop, pop of the regulars.'* Presumably the Prince Regent did not recognise his graphic tormentor there in the rank and file, as they paraded past him, or there might have been less happy memories of that glamorous occasion.

The Loyal North Britons were disbanded after the Review, only to be hastily summoned back to the colours when news arrived of Napoleon's escape from Elba. After Waterloo the Government decided that the peace in Europe was permanent, recalled all rifles and brought George's soldiering to a summary end – at least for another forty years. The peace at home, however, was to prove disturbingly fragile.

3 Radicals and Royalists
(1815-1821)

The years that immediately followed the triumph over Napoleon were stirring – not to say dangerous – times to be a Radical in London. The summer of 1814 saw the capital in festive mood: Hyde Park was the setting for a victory extravaganza of fireworks, mock battles and lavish entertainments that degenerated into a week-long drunken debauch that resisted all the authorities' efforts to break it up. Glittering processions of Allied princes and grand dukes, self-congratulating and condescending, passed through the metropolis on their way to wine and dine at Carlton House. (Cruikshank captured the irony of the situation in his 'Russian Condescension or the Blessings of Universal Peace', where he pictures the Czar and his sister stopping their carriage to distribute cakes to the children of starving English peasants.) It might have seemed that Britain's material prosperity was as well-founded and substantial as Nash's monumental thoroughfare that was rising south of Piccadilly Circus. If so, it was an illusion.

Foreign subsidies to bankrupt European states and the cost of maintaining wars in Spain and America had inflated the National Debt to dizzying proportions. Peninsular War veterans, returning penniless to the homes some of them had not seen since 1808, would barely have recognised the land they had left. Even in the year of Waterloo, unemployment in the towns was accelerating, and a desperate recession on the land was soon driving workers to seek vengeance in a spate of rick-burning. Industry, no longer on a war-footing, was over producing, business was paralysed and the commodity markets falling. The income tax – which successive governments had promised would last only as long as the war – showed no signs whatever of disappearing. The cruellest blow for the working-man, however, was the exorbitant price of his bread, kept artificially high by legislation excluding foreign corn from these shores until the homegrown commodity reached eighty shillings a quarter. To the Tories in government the Corn Act, passed in March 1815, appeared the most plausible means of revitalising agriculture (and thus protecting their own landed interests). To the man in the street who had cheerfully borne the exigencies of the war, this first act of peace was an intolerable burden, a renewal of the tyranny of an antediluvian parliament. Even as the Bill was passing, in spite of a flood of petitions,

22

through the House, George was busy at work on a print for Fores of Piccadilly, 'The Blessings of Peace or the Curse of the Corn Bill', which summed up the popular spirit of resentment. In it a boatload of foreigners are jettisoning sackfuls of corn ('the best for 50s.') into the sea, having been turned back by a group of country gentlemen who refuse to have the corn 'at any price'.

Many poor families sought their 'freedom' in the young colonies: but a more immediate reaction was the bitter groundswell of public indignation that erupted into violence in the streets of London. Parliament was beseiged by chanting mobs. Ministers found their houses broken into and sacked. The Radicals, whose political voice had been all but silenced by twenty years of war, suddenly regained a focus for their offensive on parliamentary reform. The hated Corn Act and its progenitors were assailed on radical platforms up and down the country, in handbills and tracts that mushroomed mysteriously in the streets, and nowhere more vehemently than in William Cobbett's twopenny paper *The Political Register*, which was very soon selling 50,000 copies a week. Radical clubs were re-born, and a new generation of reforming heroes emerged, like Henry Hunt the 'Orator'.

If the government spies who noted down every inflammatory utterance of these agitators hoped that time would cool these passions, they misjudged the time – and the weather. The summer of 1816 was the worst in living memory, its sullen downpours deepening the depression and hardening the reformers' resolve. By the end of the year the price of wheat had reached one hundred and three shillings, and outbreaks of vandalism and machine-breaking were becoming frequent in industrial towns all over the north of England. In London, mass meetings denounced the landed oligarchs in Parliament, and resolved to petition the Prince Regent as a last resort. One such meeting, at Spa Fields in December, ignited into hysteria, then the looting of gunsmiths' shops (and the murder of one shopkeeper), culminating in an abortive call to march, Bastille-fashion, on the Tower of London. At the opening of Parliament two months later the Regent – long inured to the hissing and booing of the crowds – actually found his carriage being pelted with missiles.

The instincts and reactions of Lord Liverpool's government were still firmly rooted in the eighteenth century: the spectre of Paris in 1789 still lurked in their minds, along with the conviction that they had not defeated the revolutionary armies of France simply to surrender to the threats of a reforming rabble. Their response was unsophisticated but effective in the short term. Habeas Corpus was suspended, magistrates given wide powers to deal with the crisis, and special constables enrolled. Cobbett contrived to evade the wave of arrests that followed by escaping to America: among those less fortunate was the publisher and bookseller, William Hone.

Hone was a social reformer, whose political views had been moulded in the cloak-and-dagger school of the London Corresponding Society, whose lectures he had attended (with no little risk to himself) as a young lad in the 1790s. Leading members of the society had later been tried as revolutionaries, but William Hone's radicalism was altogether gentler and – by his own admission – more quixotic. His earliest project, a kind of savings and insurance scheme for the poor, rapidly went bankrupt, leaving him and his family of seven destitute. Misfortune seems to have been the hallmark of subsequent commercial adventures too: a spell as an auctioneer ended in insolvency, and the small secondhand book shop which alone stood between him and the workhouse was broken into no less than three times.

Hone's first serious foray into publishing came in 1815, the same year in which his celebrated collaboration with Cruikshank began. There is every reason to think that George had known William Hone, twelve years his senior, for some time before that and a print in *The Scourge* of November 1811 shows Hone in the company of George and Robert Cruikshank ('Interior View of the House of God'). Hone's tiny bookshop at 55 Fleet Street was but a few steps away from the family home in Dorset Street, and a natural meeting-place for dissidents, reformers and radicals of various hues. Looking back on his youth, George supposed himself to have been 'rather radical' at the time, though his political beliefs must have appeared somewhat nebulous to Hone, who was an active campaigner on the Liberals' behalf. What the two men undoubtedly shared was an intuitive mistrust of the Establishment, an inherited distaste for Popery, and a natural humanitarianism.

Their association, and their subsequent success, was founded on a strong personal friendship. There was a tradition in the Hone family that the portly, well-intentioned bookseller had consciously sought to take George under his wing when the artist's father had died (in 1811): and indeed an unmistakably paternal note creeps often into Hone's accounts of his protégé. Thus he wrote, a little later, to Cruikshank's mother: 'Whatever of kindness I entertain, and I entertain much, for your son George, has been from admiration of his talents and respect for his honourable disposition.'* Anything, he went on, that diminished these qualities evoked from him not just regret, but actually caused him 'to remonstrate with him more severely than anyone but a sincere friend, feeling deeply for his best interests and real welfare, would venture to do'. This concern for George's welfare extended to keeping open house – after they moved into more spacious premises at Ludgate Hill in 1817 – for the young man, in an effort to keep him off the streets. 'Both our mother and father [one of Hone's daughters recalled] sought to draw him from the loose companionship he indulged in, by keeping him at home in the evenings.'*

George, for his part, was a frequent visitor to the family circle – the memory of grandfather Hone's long homilies on Cromwell and the Scottish Covenanters remained with him for the rest of his life – and often he would stay there the whole night. George was the only guest Mrs Hone ever had a bed made up for. In William Hone he recognised a man 'deeply read in theological questions . . . whose conduct was regulated by the strictest morality',* and he was ready and willing to be summoned to work at all hours whenever Hone was gripped by some crusading zeal.

As a member of a voluntary committee inspecting conditions in lunatic asylums, for instance, William Hone was appalled by the case of William Norris, an American who had been literally riveted alive in iron bonds at Bethlehem Hospital so that for twelve years he had been unable to move even twelve inches from the wall of his cell. As a young lad George had listened fascinated to his father's horrified account of a visit to that same hospital,* and the etched portrait of Norris he now produced for Hone to publish is an uncompromising comment on man's inhumanity. It took another twenty years for these brutal mechanical restraints to be abolished, but that sombre cell in Bethlehem marked a significant milestone in the cause.

Not all the fruits of their partnership were quite so high-minded. During 1816 three Cruikshank caricatures appeared in Hone's catalogue, all of them directed against the Regent, and accompanied by verses from Hone himself. The prints in question were 'Hone's View of the Regent's Bomb, now uncovered for the gratification of the Public'; 'Saluting the Regent's Bomb uncovered on his Birthday'; and 'The Yacht for the R . . . . t's B.m.'. It had just so happened that, to mark their joint victories over the usurper Napoleon, the King of Spain had presented the Prince with a monstrous mortar-cannon. This celebrated Bomb – pronounced bum – furnished the cartoonists with countless ribald points of comparison with the Regent's own generous anatomy. Such royal facetiousness was all grist to George's mill: for Hone they were unusual excursions into low satire. Yet, ironically, when another assault on the throne was planned it was George who declined – or perhaps was not invited – to have anything to do with it, fortunately for him as it turned out.

By the end of 1816 the temper of the people and the intransigence of Parliament was making a confrontation imminent. The success of Cobbett's *Register* testified to the unprecedented power of the printing-press in crystallising opinion; and already a veritable army of radical hawkers could be mustered to distribute the word. Politically it was the time for Hone to enter the lists – though his enemies always maintained he did so with an eye for a quick turnover. The first of Hone's satires appeared in January 1817, a witty, scalding attack on the Ministry and the Regent. 'Catechism of a Ministerial Member' was a faithful parody of the Church catechism, supposedly 'to be learned of every person before he be brought to be confirmed as Placeman by the Minister'. The Articles of Belief began:

> I believe in George, the Regent Almighty, Maker of New Streets and Knights of the Bath; and in the present ministry, his only choice, who were conceived of Toryism ... were execrated, dead and buried. In a few months ... they re-ascended to the Treasury Benches, and sit at the right hand of a little man in a large wig; from whence they laugh at the petitions of the people ....

The Commandments and the Lord's Prayer are similarly travestied, sparing no 'pensioner, placeman, expectant parasite, toadeater or Lord of the Bedchamber'.

Strangely – for he was no great churchman nor respecter of politicians – George was perturbed by what his friend had done. No sooner was the 'Catechism' out on the streets than he was begging Hone to withdraw the pamphlet immediately 'for that it would bring great odium upon him from all respectable people'.* More to the point, it was his opinion that 'the Government would certainly prosecute'. It is hard to believe that Cruikshank was shocked (as some have suggested) by the mere fact that the Church's liturgy had been parodied, since he himself penned equally harsh paragraphs on the Church (at least that of Rome) later in life. Hone, apparently, did not share his misgivings, for in quick succession two more religious parodies were published under his name, 'The Political Litany' ('From an unnational debt, from unmerited pensions and sinecure places, from an extravagant civil list, and from utter starvation – Good Prince, deliver us!') and 'The Sinecurist's Creed' based on the Athanasian Creed.

At the end of February the Government moved to suspend Habeas Corpus and, informed that the existence of 'blasphemous parodies' was specifically cited in the Act on which the suspension was to be founded, Hone took the better part of valour and withdrew his tracts from circulation. At first it seemed as if his prudence had saved him from prosecution – in spite of a new-found role as editor of *The Reformists' Register* – yet on 3 May he was apprehended by two men in Fleet Lane, who produced a warrant for his arrest, refused him leave to return home and summarily deposited him in jail. There he remained for two months before being released on bail to prepare for his trial. George, meanwhile, regardless of the ubiquitous informers, took up his friend's cause unreservedly: he even dictated a letter to the Attorney-General himself, begging him not to start proceedings, and had it delivered to his home by one of Hone's small sons. That august official, though in the middle of shaving, consented to admit the lad and read the plea. Quite what he made of that strange missive, from an advocate as unruly as Cruikshank, is not recorded, but Hone's indictment went ahead nevertheless.

Much of that autumn was taken up with the impending trial: the *Register* was wound up, and Hone began to build up his defence – reportedly with the artist's help – often dropping into George's studio to rehearse parts of his speech. The strains of anticipation were taking a toll on the publisher's health, though clearly not on his morale, as several ministers discovered from the trenchant little squibs about them, all embellished with Cruikshank caricatures, that kept popping up from 55 Fleet Street. On the morning of the trial, 18 December, an animated crowd surrounded the Guildhall where Hone arrived in his shabbiest suit and preceded by a small library of dusty books. The prosecution clearly expected an easy victory; but they had misjudged their man, his great store of knowledge and sense of occasion. He had not, he insisted, parodied the rites of the Church of England for which no man in the court had greater respect than he: he had merely used the forms to parody another object – just as Luther had done. And as he produced his list of former parodists – Milton, Latimer, the then Dean of Canterbury, Gillray, even George Canning, a member of the Cabinet – none of whom had ever been prosecuted, the Government began to find the ground cut from under its feet. The jury thought so too, and acquitted Hone in fifteen minutes.

The Attorney-General, however, was not finished with him. The next day Hone was brought before the court, presided over by the Lord Chief Justice himself (seemingly determined to gain a conviction), to answer for his second tract, 'The Litany'. Once again he was acquitted and, amid mounting excitement, again on the third day when the last of his parodies was prosecuted. For a moment Hone was the most celebrated man in London, champion of the jubilant Radicals – for no one doubted that the charge of 'blasphemy' was only window-dressing for a political trial. A fund to alleviate Hone's monetary distress – his children, he said, had not slept in sheets for months – was soon subscribed to £3,000. Nor was George the man to pass up a profitable opportunity: within the space of a few days he had etched for Fores a series of celebratory satires. In 'Great Gobble, Gobble, Gobble' his friend, as Tom Tit, sits on a farmyard fence haranguing a gaggle of geese (his persecutors) and a most discountenanced turkey (the Lord Chief Justice).

For almost two years after the trials George appears to have done very little work for Hone, beyond the odd frontispiece. The problem was that the publisher, still enfeebled by his ordeal, had determined to forsake pamphleteering in favour of a more respectable, substantial form of publishing. Yet the one exception, the 'Bank Restriction Note' in which both men had a hand, proved to be the most memorable of

27

all their output during this period. It was an imaginative piece of work by any yardstick, and one of which George remained justifiably proud all his life – although his claims for it as an instrument of social reform were perhaps exaggerated by the passage of time. Reid's Catalogue dates the 'Bank Restriction Note' at 1820, which would make nonsense of Cruikshank's later claim that it had appeared before Peel's Act for the resumption of cash payments (in July 1819). Indeed, an advertisement in *The Times* shows beyond doubt that the print was published on 26 January 1819.

One of the myriad of petty offences that in those days still incurred the death penalty was the forging of currency notes. Worse still, the mere act of passing a counterfeit note was sufficient to send a man to the gallows; and many a man and woman went, for not only was there an extraordinary number of banknotes in circulation (since the Bank of England had suspended cash payments in 1797), they were absurdly easy to imitate, being cheaply produced and coarsely etched. In spite of the extreme punishment the temptation was clearly great, since some 18,000 forged notes at least had been presented in 1816. The 'Bank Restriction Note' was a broad, not particularly subtle, take-off of one such banknote, and the inspiration for it came to George one morning in 1818 during a visit to a house near the Bank of England.

> . . . in returning home between eight and nine o'clock down Ludgate Hill, and seeing a number of persons looking up the Old Bailey, I looked that way myself, and saw several human beings hanging on the gibbet opposite Newgate prison, and to my horror two of these were women; and upon enquiring what these women had been hung for, was informed that it was for passing forged one-pound notes. The fact that a poor woman could be put to death for such a minor offence had a great effect on me – and I at that moment determined, if possible, to put a stop to this shocking destruction of life for merely obtaining a few shillings by fraud; and well knowing the habits of the low class of society in London, I felt quite sure that in very many cases the rascals who forged the notes induced these poor women to go into the gin-shops to 'get something to drink' and thus *pass* the notes, and hand them the change.*

When he returned home to Dorset Street George immediately sat down to sketch a 'Banknote not to be imitated', which was lying on the table when half an hour later William Hone dropped in. He saw the sketch, was much taken with it and offered to publish it. And so he did, neatly sealed in its own envelope together with a page of text ('The Bank Restriction Barometer') elucidating the economic and social advantages of restoring gold currency. When the print first appeared in Hone's new shop-window on Ludgate Hill it caused a great sensation, George recorded, drawing such a crowd that the Lord Mayor had to send in the City police to disperse them. The printing of the 'Notes' (at a shilling each) could not keep up with public demand, and the artist had to sit up all night etching a second plate: the publisher, George records – slightly ruefully, for he had no commission on the work – cleared £700 on this enterprise.

Many years later, when Cruikshank's obituarists were noting the 'Bank Restriction Note' among some of his most celebrated pieces, one of Hone's sons publicly made the claim that it had in fact been his father's work. The 'Barometer' was, of course, but there is no evidence to show he made any significant contribution to the 'Note'. (Hackwood in his *Life of Hone* (1912) reproduces a rough sketch of this print dated 12 January 1819, which was 'supposed to show Hone's pencillings'. In fact the pencil writing on this sketch is unquestionably Cruikshank's.) A more vexed question is the validity of George's own claim that the print was directly responsible for the abolition of the death sentence for forgery. 'I consider it the most important design and etching that I ever made in my life,' he once confided to a correspondent, 'for it has saved the lives of thousands of my fellow-creatures.' The route by which he reached this magnificent conclusion he explains as follows:

> The Bank directors held a meeting immediately [after publication] on the subject, and *after that* they issued no more one-pound notes, and so there was no more hanging for passing forged one-pound notes; not only that, but ultimately no hanging, even for forgery. *After this* Sir Robert Peel got a Bill passed in Parliament for the 'Resumption of cash payments'. *After this* he revised the Penal Code, and *after that* there was not any more hanging or punishment of DEATH for minor offences.

It is not that George's chronology is at fault – although the Bank had as a matter of fact made a partial resumption of cash payments in October 1817 – it is that he fails to recognise any motive link between these events other than the 'Bank Restriction Note'. He takes no account of the mounting body of informed opinion, inside Parliament and out, that was already pressing for an end to these and similar injustices, and in particular he ignores the efforts of Sir Samuel Romilly who had actually steered a Bill to that effect through the Commons in 1816 – only to have it thrown out by the Lords.

It won't do, though, to condemn George out of hand for deliberate misrepresentation, as many have done. The arts of satire and caricature are elusive ones, their effects (if any) intangible but none the less potent for that. Perhaps George III did dismiss North after seeing one of Townshend's cartoons, as one newspaper suggested; perhaps Charles James Fox did lose more votes in the House through the cartoons of

Sayers than through the speeches of the Opposition, as he himself claimed. Who knows? More than any other cartoonist Cruikshank desperately *wanted* his work to change people's minds and, increasingly as he got older, believed in a moralistic view of his art. His real shortcoming was to suppose he actually *had* influenced people's opinions, and even that has to be judged in the light of the undisputed fact that in those early months of 1819 the 'Bank Restriction Note' was what we would describe nowadays as a runaway best-seller, a vivid piece of propaganda and a constant topic of conversation. And before the year was out George, and his friend William Hone, were to be even more firmly welded to the reformists' cause in the public's mind.

1818 had shown a discernible, if hardly dramatic, improvement in the nation's economic plight: and politically the Government's heavy hand seemed to have tempered the worst radical excesses sufficiently for a general election to be held with only the normal amount of tumult, and for Habeas Corpus to be reinstated. But it was an uneasy truce, the administration stubbornly entrenched in its policies, the Radicals truculently biding their time. And it only needed the renewed recession of 1819 to expose again the gulf of resentment that separated the poor from the rich. Wages plummeted once more and factories fell silent, only this time no one was to be persuaded that this was one of the natural consequences of the aftermath of war.

Ominously, the revolutionary slogans reappeared, the liberty caps, mass rallies in Birmingham, Leeds and other northern centres. To apprehensive magistrates the speeches seemed as inflammatory as the stifling heat of that summer; men of property observed the unemployed drilling with sharpened staves and resolved to defend themselves. The flash-point came on 16 August, when an army of reformers assembled on St Peter's Field, Manchester, more than fifty thousand marching to the beat of drums. The local magistrates maintained that stones were thrown: the Radicals insisted the yeomanry were sent in without cause to arrest Henry Hunt. At all events there were scuffles, the yeomanry panicked and drew their sabres. Hundreds were cut down or crushed; eleven, including two women, died. Afterwards the field looked like a battleground – and it came to be known for all time as the battle of Peterloo.

Wellington expected the people to rise up in vengeance, and recruited ten thousand new troops in anticipation. Nor did the Regent go out of his way to placate the howls of indignation, communicating to the Manchester authorities his 'great satisfaction . . . for their prompt, decisive and efficient measures'. But, in spite of the grinding of scythes and hardening of attitudes (an estimated 300,000 people greeted Hunt's arrival in London in September), there was no insurrection, for the leadership was not unanimously committed to violence nor – in the end – equal to it. But English blood had been spilt, and the conscience of liberal men was profoundly disturbed by the thought. Even William Hone, by now totally absorbed in his magnum opus *The History of Parody*, was moved to protest.

Hone's inspiration did not come for nearly three months until, he says, one day he observed one of his little daughters looking at the pictures in a children's book. It was *The House that Jack Built*, and 'an idea flashed across my mind – I saw at once the use that might be made of it'. It was a happy thought (though, truth to tell, one that had already been used in the *Manchester Observer* shortly after the massacre), for the Government would look even sillier objecting to a nursery-book than it did inveighing against a prayer-book parody.

Yet 'The Political House that Jack Built' was an incisive lampoon, setting out the cause of reform for even the most unlettered. Jack's house (the political institutions of the nation) and its wealth (the people's rights), so the scenario runs, have been plundered by vermin (the military, the law, the church, the politicians). But

> *This is THE THING that, in spite of new Acts,*
> *And attempts to restrain it, by soldiers or tax,*
> *Will poison the Vermin*
> *That plunder the wealth,*
> *That lay in the House*
> *That Jack built.*

It is indeed a printing-press. But then we are introduced to the enemy of the Press (the public informer) and his 'reasons of lawless power' (the yeomanry), and then the source of this power:

> *This is THE MAN – all shaven and shorn,*
> *All cover'd with Orders – and all forlorn*
> *THE DANDY OF SIXTY, who bows with a grace,*
> *And has taste in wigs, collars, cuirasses and lace.*

And thus the counterpoint of good (the people, reform) and evil (the ministers, clerical magistrates) is played out to the end.

The text was already written when George was called in to illustrate the verses. Hone read them aloud to him, striking extempore attitudes to suit each character and, apparently, even rehearsing the artist in likenesses he was unfamiliar with. Be that as it may, Cruikshank's woodcuts catch the spirit of the parody admirably, broad-lined, naïve almost, guaranteed to recall the crude chap-books of the reader's youth. Indeed, there were wicked voices later heard abroad suggesting that the pamphlet's success was due entirely to George's drawings:

> *For who, in fits at Cruiky's droll designs,*
> *Can stay to criticise lop-sided rhymes?*

wrote one fellow-parodist. He advised the publisher to take good care of George, for should he once decide to take up writing on his own account:

> *Your libels then would sell about as quick, Sir,*
> *As bare quack labels would without th'elixir.*
> *Were Cruikshank wise, he might with trouble small,*
> *Write his own labels, and eclipse you all.*

But Hone could afford to shrug off such sour grapes, for by March the pamphlet was in its fifty-second edition having sold upwards of 100,000 copies. Its popularity stung the loyalists to publish their own rejoinder, 'The Constitutional House that Jack Built', whose fawning illustrations served only to emphasise the universal appeal of Cruikshank's deceptively artless portraits: his plumed and bemedalled Regent ('the dandy of sixty') and the despairing huddle of working-men ('all tatter'd and torn') in particular.

In December 1819, the Government, doubtless relieved to have survived so long without a general call to arms, tightened its grip on the situation with six new Acts. These notorious measures banned unauthorised 'military' training and public meetings, permitted search without warrant, increased duty on cheap periodicals, and drastically extended magistrates' powers in respect of sedition and libel. 'The Political House' was not affected by the new stamp duty since it was already priced at one shilling (or three shillings coloured on vellum paper), but inevitably its contents came under the scrutiny of the Privy Council. Hone recorded that the Prince Regent examined it in silence, laid it on the table without comment and departed. The Council – perhaps taking this as some sort of guideline – decided they had had enough of prosecuting William Hone and quietly buried the matter.

The Six Acts, all the same, bit deep into the radical movement: within a very few months radical leaders like Hunt and Sir Francis Burdett, publishers like Carlile and Wooler (owner of *The Black Dwarf*) and dozens of other reformers had been imprisoned after one of the most relentless legal purges in history. Cruikshank was swift to register his disgust. In mid-December his 'Free Born Englishman' was already on display at Fores', showing this poor downtrodden creature with mouth padlocked, hands tied, feet manacled and surrounded by all the symbols of his repression – the debtor's prison, the axe of the libel laws and so on. This print was based on an earlier Cruikshank (1813) of the same title, protesting at the imprisonment of Leigh Hunt for libel. Also in mid-December, another blast by Cruikshank was published by Tegg, 'Poor Bull and his Burden', which carries echoes of 'The Political House'. The Bull (the people) is prostrated by the same 'vermin' as in the pamphlet.

The libel laws did not deter Hone from capitalising on the astonishing success of 'The Political House'; within six weeks another satire was on the streets, this time a send-up of the Prince Regent's bellicose Speech from the Throne at the opening of Parliament in November 1819. 'The Man in the Moon' was set in the mythical kingdom of Lunataria, whose 'senate' nevertheless was uncannily similar to the gathering at Westminster and whose inhabitants – as portrayed in George's several woodcuts – were eminently identifiable. By a strange coincidence the ruler of Lunataria, like the Regent on earth, also had a father in the final throes of mental derangement – as he signifies at the beginning of his speech:

> *My L.rds and G..tl...n,*
> *I grieve to say,*
> *That poor old Dad,*
> *Is just as – bad,*
> *As when I met you here*
> *the other day.*

Within two months 'The Man in the Moon' had reached its twenty-sixth edition and, like its predecessor, inspired a host of imitations. In a note on the last page Hone had warned his readers that this was 'possibly his very last production' of such a nature 'owing to imperative claims upon his pen of a higher order' (presumably his history of parody). But even as 'The Man in the Moon' was coming off the press, events were conspiring to confound that particular prophecy.

At the end of January 1820 'poor old Dad', the mindless and forgotten George III, died and 'the dandy of sixty' at long last became George IV. This joyful elevation – for which he had waited none too patiently since the first signs of his father's illness more than thirty years before – was soured from the start by the news that his long-estranged wife, Princess Caroline, was returning from her self-imposed exile on the Continent to take up her rightful place as his Queen. It had required a bottle of brandy to get the Prince to the altar to marry this vociferous lady in the first place, and though she had born him a daughter (who had died in 1817) he had never treated her as a wife, still less a princess. In 1806 he had had her 'investigated' on suspicion of having had an illegitimate child – fruitlessly as it turned out, except that a few years later she mercifully took herself off to Europe and out of his life. There, so his spies across the water informed him, she made ostentatious progresses from one capital to another, making little effort to conceal her indiscretions. Another investigation was begun in 1817, with a view to extracting from a motley collection of Italian witnesses sufficient evidence for a divorce; but such was the procrastination of this 'commission' that no proceedings had been started by the time the old King died.

In this vendetta the Prince had little public sympathy. The people thought Caroline grossly ill-used, the very epitome of marital virtue when compared with the flagrant derelictions of her husband and his train of grandmaternal mistresses. She was, moreover, an uncomfortable political weapon in the hands of Whigs, Radicals and others, used to beat him and Liverpool's ministry which was reluctantly supporting his plans for divorce. The furore that followed Princess Caroline's inconvenient decision to return to England and which absorbed the country for the rest of the year was thus animated by a variety of passions. Thackeray would have it that Cruikshank's involvement in the affair was motivated by moral indignation:

> . . . he most certainly believed [he wrote in retrospect] that the Princess was the most spotless, pure-mannered darling of a princess that ever married a heartless debauchee of a Prince Royal . . . . Cruikshank could not stand by and see a woman ill-used, and so struck in for her rescue, he and the people belabouring with all their might the party who were making the attack, and determining from pure sympathy and indignation, that the woman must be innocent because her husband had treated her so foully.*

That Caroline was such a paragon – or that George necessarily believed her to be – must be doubted, but her support from the bulk of the Press (and the radical wing in particular) was assured. Hone apparently was reluctant at first to get involved, being at the time 'out of the way of politics, about which my mind had begun to misgive me', but some of the Queen's friends bearded him in the British Museum one day and persuaded him to write something on her behalf.

The result, 'The Queen's Matrimonial Ladder', was offered for sale shortly before the Queen's 'trial' opened in mid-August. It was based on a popular plaything (called a matrimonial ladder), with each rung of the ladder representing an episode in the sorry

34

history of the royal marriage, including the Prince's amorous adventures, the Princess's humiliations culminating in the Bill of Pains and Penalties, the instrument by which she was to be divorced and stripped of her titles. Each of the fourteen episodes was illustrated by a telling woodcut by George, some of them surpassing even the *Scourge* for sheer vituperation. The new King is portrayed as a tattered spendthrift pleading with his father, as an officious Charley informing on his wife, as (yet again) the bloated Prince of Whales, as a pot-bellied Guy Fawkes – and the final indignity, as 'Cat's meat', a pile of flesh being trundled off in a wheelbarrow in the hope of a sale. Most memorable of all is the first plate, with the Prince in his cups sprawled amongst the litter of his drinking and gambling. It is, in effect, an evocation of Gillray's famous 'Voluptuary under the horrors of Digestion' but without a shred of the dignity Gillray had allowed his Prince. Cruikshank's figure has passed the point of no return, dissipation etched into his features, a roué insensible to his royal squalor. It is a brilliant caricature that seems to embody all the cynicism of George's youth with an edge of morality more characteristic of his later years.

Predictably, 'The Queen's Matrimonial Ladder' was an instant success, perhaps contributing to Caroline's eventual triumph – certainly someone in office thought it worthwhile to offer Hone £500 to suppress it, to no avail. It is interesting to note that, for the first time in their collaboration, the name of George Cruikshank actually appears at the beginning of the pamphlet. Not that any informed reader could fail to have recognised George's style: rather it is a somewhat belated acknowledgement by the publisher of the artist's true contribution. For all his fatherly affection it remained Hone's opinion that George's genius 'had been wasted on mere caricature till it embodied my ideas and feelings',* by which one must assume he meant that Cruikshank needed some vision, some commitment to a clear social purpose which Hone was able to give him.

If so, it must have come as some disappointment to Hone to discover that when the Loyal Association (the King's men) riposted to his pamphlet with one of their own, 'The Radical Ladder', the frontispiece had been drawn by none other than George Cruikshank himself. The design shows the Queen, supported by a train of gnome-like Radicals, mounting a ladder and brandishing a torch with intent to burn the Crown ensconced on the top of the pillar of the Constitution. It stands in stark contrast to the pure, misused Caroline George had been depicting a few weeks earlier.

It is indeed a glaring inconsistency – though not without precedent in George's earlier work – and very likely helped Hone to his long suspicion that 'George was by no means friendly to reform'. But that would be too facile a conclusion: looking back on his youth George really did count himself among the Radicals at the time – as in fact the bulk of his political plates proclaim him to have been – and his own brother Robert made a point of including him in a sinister group of Jacobins portrayed in a violently anti-Radical cartoon of 1821, 'The Revolutionary Association'. In this same print, however, there is also a clue to George's apparent inconstancy: Robert depicts him as poring over some 'black designs', and removing his faithful pipe from his mouth in order to spit into an upturned crown doing duty as a spittoon. On the puff of smoke wafting about him are written the words 'Damn all things', which is self-evidently how his own brother analysed his political philosophy at the time. That this was the purpose of the caption is reinforced by Robert's self-portrait, just behind George. Robert represents himself as uncommitted as his brother but in a more responsible fashion: on *his* puff of smoke is written 'Much may be said on both sides'.

Yet another token of the artist's lack of allegiance in the whole sordid scandal – though whether Hone ever knew of it we shall probably never know – has survived in the Royal Archives at Windsor. It is a receipt for £100 paid to the artist, supposedly 'in consideration of a pledge not to caricature His Majesty in any immoral situation'.* Such regal hand-outs were fairly commonplace – indeed, an expensive item when one considers the torrents of abuse that were pouring down on the King from all quarters in 1820. And the precedent of 'pensioning' a cartoonist was already well-established: Sayers, Gillray, even (it is supposed) Hogarth, received their share of bribes from the Court at different times. However, this once-and-for-all payment to George smacks more of a reward than of the bribe the palace records make it out to be – for several reasons. In the first place it is a rather paltry sum if it was intended to buy silence (the more so when compared with Hone's offer of £500). And at all events George did *not* desist from lampooning the King: the receipt is dated 19 June 1820, some weeks before the appearance of 'The Queen's Matrimonial Ladder'. Much more feasible is the possibility that someone at Court had seen a mordant anti-Caroline print published by Humphrey on 15 June – and engraved by Cruikshank – and deemed it worth a speculative £100 to encourage the artist to further insults to the Queen. The satire in question, 'La Gloire des honnetes Gens!', is a series of scenes from Caroline's exile in Europe: in each of them she is dressed most immodestly and attended by the leering Bergami – the Italian adventurer who was appointed her Chamberlain and was widely assumed to be her lover. So much, then, for Thackeray's 'spotless, pure-mannered darling'.

The truth of the matter, one suspects, is that as a freelance print-maker George could scarcely afford to take sides in a royal scandal that afforded him such an abundance of material. The success of his work for Hone did not commit him irretrievably to the Queen's cause: still less did it make him a rich man. Half a guinea for a woodcut was an accepted fee in those days – though Hone does seem to have paid him at a slightly higher rate, as well he might. (For the seventy-eight plates by Cruikshank that were later re-published under the title of *Facetiae* he was paid a total of £60, according to a note in Hone's handwriting. Certainly there is no evidence for the miserliness hinted at by a writer in *Fraser's Magazine* (June 1830), who claimed that George had never received more than £18 from the publisher.) But granted he could – it was said – finish two or three blocks in one day, his precarious income in no way allowed him the luxury of turning down a commission from another print-seller for 'political' reasons.

The same unpredictability in his protégé's private life bothered Hone equally: like many other independent young men of Regency London for whom being 'fast' was fashionable, George could display a disregard for the common civilities of life that was quite deplorable at times. 'Yesterday afternoon', Hone wrote, clearly piqued, 'he [George] came to insist that I should forthwith proceed to the worthy Alderman Waithman, and get the watch-house keeper of an adjoining parish dismissed for having differed with him in opinion upon a point a few evenings ago.' When his friend quite reasonably chose not to do this, George 'sent for a pipe and blew clouds of tobacco smoke over me and my books, in my hall of Parody, for a couple of hours, demanded entrance to my wife's bedroom to shave and smarten himself for an evening party, took possession of my best Brandenburg pumps, damned me under the denomination of "Old Robin Gray" because I had not a chapeau bras, [and] otherwise discomposed the wonted order of my mind and household'.*

But then at other times young George could be as entertaining and aimiable a companion as he could be irritating. Hone cherished the memory of one of their outings together, to Islington with two other friends one May morning. It was in the nature of a last pilgrimage to Sir Walter Raleigh's old house, which was about to be demolished before the tide of advancing developers; the object, which must have appealed to George's sentimental streak, was 'to smoke a pipe in the same room that the man who first introduced tobacco smoked in himself' and to toast the immortal memory of Sir Walter. And so they did – George in truth 'smoking pipes innumerable' – and downed several pots of porter before retiring to the Pied Bull, already self-admittedly inebriated, to move on to 3/6d port wine and bowls of punch!*

Their collaboration throughout 1820 continued fertile, nourished as it was by the interminable saga of the royal divorce and apparently unimpaired by George's defection to the loyalists. Caroline's trial dragged on into the autumn, reducing its early passions into boredom and often farce: the people, though still convinced of her innocence, had tired of their demonstrations and the Lords, though still persuaded of her guilt, were confused by the dazzling rhetoric of the Queen's advocate (Brougham) and the contradictions of the wretched Italian witnesses. One of them, a Theodore Majocci – thinking perhaps to do the Queen a service – conveniently lost his memory and gave rise to much public hilarity with his refrain of '*Non mi ricordo*' (I don't remember), which became a catch-phrase all over town. Hone chose this particular incident to pillory the King yet again in his next squib, 'Non Mi Ricordo', which appeared while the trial was still in progress: as Cruikshank's frontispiece makes clear, with his now familiar flabby-jowled dandy, here it is the King who is on the witness stand. Under cross-examination on the subject of his flagrant infidelities he too, needless to say, suffers a mysterious bout of amnesia.

By 10 November, when the final reading of the Bill was passed in the Lords by a mere nine votes, even the Government had wearied of the charade and informed the King that with such a majority the Bill could not possibly be taken to the Commons. It therefore died, neither satisfying the King nor absolving the Queen, though Caroline's supporters made the best of it by celebrating her 'victory' with four days of illuminations in the City. George's contribution was an epic painted transparency which covered Hone's shopfront, surmounted by the motto 'Knowledge is power' lit up by variegated lamps. It was hauled back into position on 29 November for Caroline's benefit, so that she should observe it on her way to worship at St Paul's – a wise precaution at all events, since shopkeepers who had neglected their illuminations found all their windows broken.

The central figures of George's illumination – a portrait of the Queen flanked by Liberty and a printing-press – are irradiated by a sun-burst that banishes all manner of vermin and demons (readily identifiable as pillars of the establishment) into outer darkness. It offered in effect a whole new scenario for a satire, as artist and publisher must have realised at one of their editorial conferences at the Spotted Dog chop-house – or the Southampton Coffee-House in Chancery Lane, where George would sketch out his ideas in the ale spilled on the table. 'The Political Showman', which appeared in the spring of 1821, in time to celebrate George IV's belated coronation, is a zoological catalogue of those curious creatures 'exhibited at Court before the King' precisely as they appeared in Cruikshank's painted transparency: the scorpion Wellington, the black rats of the Solicitor- and Attorney-Generals, a masked Archbishop with his episcopal locusts, Liverpool as a broken crutch with his borough-mongering opossums, the King as a water-scorpion . . . and so on, culminating in the most horrific exhibit of all, a scaly dragon spouting blood and devouring the people. This is the Monarchy, but on closer inspection it is clearly in the last stages of decrepitude and actually stinging itself to death with its forked tail.

Hone and Cruikshank were far from the only ones who thought the monarchy had discredited itself beyond repair. Lord Bedford confided to his son that the end had come, and noble lords were stopped by armed pickets in the street and forced to drink the Queen's health. The King himself, humiliated beyond endurance, lived like a recluse in Windsor Park and no one even contemplated looking to his surviving brothers, the Royal Dukes, as unregenerate a bunch as you could hope to find.

But nothing happened. For the Radicals the moment had passed for the time being: the men who would have marched two years earlier were back in the factories, their leaders almost all in prison. The London crowds, their summer fever abated, forsook Caroline as capriciously as they had espoused her – and sensing this the anti-radical Press once more took the offensive. 'We thee implore, to go away and sin no more,' one pamphlet advised the Queen. 'But if that effort be too great, To go away at any rate.' She would have been well advised, for hers was the final indignity: to find herself locked out of her husband's coronation and her one-time supporters unaccountably failing to press her claims. She survived her downfall by just a fortnight. Hone persevered against the prevailing tide (notably with *A Slap at Slop* (1822), an attack on the reactionary Stoddart, editor of the anti-reform *New Times*. It took the form of a mock-newspaper complete with advertisements, and *The Examiner* claimed it to be 'the richest of all Hone's publications'), but his aim was distracted by a libel action brought against him for his 'Non Mi Ricordo', under the auspices of the newly formed Constitutional Association. This voluntary society, taking up where the authorities had abdicated, was dedicated to the ruination of all radical publishers, and though its prosecution against Hone got nowhere it had some minor triumphs against lesser militants.

'A mood of rebellion had been created by parodies, prints, caricatures, ribaldry and ridicule' the *Loyalist Magazine* pronounced. But for the moment the danger was past and, though it might not have been realised, an era was passing. The political temperature was dropping and bitterness receding: after 1822 Hone virtually retired from the political arena to immerse himself once more in the past. George too, though more concerned with the present, began to lose interest in the humdrum proceedings down at St Stephen's and even in his royal victim, who now remained cloistered for long periods in his hunting lodge finding his consolation in laudanum and Lady Conyngham. But in London itself, beyond whose horizons Cruikshank's eye was rarely tempted to stray, there were changes afoot.

4 Life in London
(1821-1830)

In one of his more self-deprecating moods George Cruikshank suggested his 'caricatures and other prints might be taken as a curious sort of pictorial illustration of the habits, manners, fashions and political feelings of the nation . . .'. There are some artists who can stand aloof, observe their times with some kind of artistic detachment. George was not one of them – whatever he may later have claimed. Confronted in his old age with examples of his more youthful work he would admit to authorship 'with regret', not because of any technical deficiency but because they were clearly the products of what a mid-Victorian would consider a disreputable age. London under the Regency, and for the decade that followed, *was* spectacularly disreputable, a stimulating, turbulent, often vicious and dangerous place to live. Until the age of twenty-nine George lived in the very heart of it, in the maze-like environs of Fleet Street (then as yet unappropriated by the newspaper presses) with the brothels of Covent Garden to the west of him, the gin-shops of the waterfront to the east. The raw material for his sketches was all around him, and because he was a part of it he could convey the grotesque beauty of it, the good-natured humanity amid the squalor.

He was not blind to the miseries and cruelties of that hand-to-mouth existence, but because he had rubbed shoulders with it from his very childhood he could isolate the incongruous, the eccentric, the whimsical – all the elements that give his sketches their animation. He describes one particular scene, when he was a young man in Fleet Street, that caught his fancy and (so he said) laid the foundations for many of his studies from life in later years:

> There was in the neighbourhood in which I resided a low public-house; it has since degenerated into a gin-palace. It was frequented by coal-heavers only, and it stood in Wilderness Lane. To this house of inelegant resort, which I regularly passed in my way to and from the Temple, my attention was one night especially attracted by the sounds of a fiddle, together with other indications of festivity; when, glancing towards the tap-room window, I could plainly discern a small bust of Shakespeare placed over the chimney-piece, with a short pipe stuck in its mouth.
> This was not clothing the palpable and the familiar with golden ex-

40

halations from the dawn, but it was reducing the glorious and immortal beauty of Apollo himself to a level with the commonplace and the vulgar. Yet there was something not to be quarrelled with in the association of ideas to which that object led. It struck me to be the perfection of the human picturesque. It was a palpable meeting of the sublime and the ridiculous . . . . I thought of what the great poet had himself been, of the parts that he had played, and the wonders he had wrought within a stone's throw of that very spot; and feeling that even he might have well wished to be there, the pleased spectator of that lower world, it was impossible not to recognise the fitness of the pipe.

What a picture of life was there! It was as though Death were dead! It was *all* life. In simpler words, I saw on approaching the window and peeping between the short red curtains a swarm of jolly coal-heavers! Coal-heavers all – save a few of the fairer and softer sex – all enjoying the hour with an intensity not to be disputed, and in a manner singularly characteristic of the tastes and propensies of aristocratic and fashionable society . . . . The living Shakespeare, had he been there, would but have seen a common humanity working out its objects.*

Coal-heavers, dustmen (especially dustmen), sailors, prostitutes, cabbies were all as integral a part of George's canvas as were the fops, dandies, courtesans, dukes, princes and prime ministers. The two Londons lived side by side, if not always in peaceful co-existence, then at least with a working acceptance of their situations, which were, if anything, being emphasised by the transformation of the city landscape.

High Life and Low Life was perhaps an over-simplified vision of society, nevertheless both formed genuinely recognisable strands in George's work (and found an echo, fifty years on, in Doré's 'paradise' and 'inferno'). The West End – the habitat of High Life (Beau Brummel claimed never to have gone further east than the Strand) – was rapidly being translated into one of the ornaments of Europe, with John Nash's colonnaded and stuccoed thoroughfare cutting a swathe from Carlton House to Marylebone Park, Decimus Burton's porticoed terraces and monumental arches, Smirke's churches and theatres, Rennie's bridges. Under influential contractors, like Burton and Cubitt, great aristocratic estates were blossoming – in Bloomsbury up to the very edges of St Pancras village and, after Buckingham Palace threatened to become the pivot of high society, in Belgravia. Nash's efforts to meet the King's extravagant demands over the reconstruction of Buckingham House were thwarted by Government economies, and became the subject of one of George's most famous satires. There were still inconvenient anomalies, it was true: in the Haymarket farmers still haggled over the price of hay while their great waggons blocked the street, and what was to become Trafalgar Square – technically still part of the royal mews – was a wasteland except for a solitary hackney stand. But one could scarcely afford not to be seen in a box at the reconstructed King's Theatre, or shopping in the new Burlington Arcade or – above all – riding in one's carriage through Hyde Park at the fashionable hour of five o'clock. Here George must have strolled for hours, drinking in the absurdities of fashion daily paraded for mutual inspection: the swallow-tail coats and Cossack trousers, flowery cravats and leg-of-mutton sleeves, Hessian boots and coal-scuttle hats – all documented in detail in the series of 'Monstrosities'.

Appearances, in this tightly knit sector of society, were everything: poise towards one's equals, condescension to one's inferiors, equanimity in the face of ruin at the faro table, and of course taste in all things. The farce that is a recurring element in George's observation of the *ton* of society consists very often in the breakdown of these 'appearances' under sheer force of circumstances, when the mask of gentility slips to reveal a human being beneath. In 'Inconveniences of a Crowded Drawing-Room' the fashionable crush – which one hostess complained was so great that all decorum vanished and 'people's clothes are literally torn to pieces' – has reduced the cream of fashion to a bitching rout. Again, the pleasures of riding in one of the newly imported 'cabs' could be, and no doubt often were, diminished by the perils of the traffic, as in 'The Comforts of a Cabriolet!' Here three such vehicles incompetently driven by some swells have come into violent collision, disgorging their occupants in humiliating fashion.

But George's special derision is reserved for the dandies, on whose façades many hours of the day and small fortunes had been lavished (not that many of them ever actually paid their tailors). Their airs and affectations were bad enough, but their proprietory claims to the pavement would have vexed a saint: lesser-clad mortals were expected to give way in their path, and the fate of those who failed to is spelled out in, amongst other prints, 'The Art of Walking the Streets of London'.

If the dandies gained their effect by, as it were, existing on their own rarefied plane, there was another species of society whose lifestyle was distinctly down-to-earth. These were the bucks or bloods (or rakes), whose endless search for diversion frequently took them into the most dissolute corners of the town, the gin-shops and whore-houses, the illegal cockpits and prize-rings, and the other piquant pleasures of the Low Life. As often as not these excursions might end with their being summarily relieved of their cash, but to a generation brought up on the merits of 'hard living' their escapades also became invested with a certain glamour.

George as a young man, according to the gossipy Henry Vizetelly, fancied himself as a bit of a buck, dressing as nattily as his income allowed, meticulously oiling his hair and brushing his whiskers and 'stealthily eyeing himself in the glass on every available opportunity'.* In vain did Hone, in his fatherly fashion, remonstrate with him at his loose living. If only (he wrote):

> ... my friend Cruikshank will forswear late hours, blue ruin [gin] and dollies – all of which united are unfriendly to certain mechanical motions of the spirit, which I tell George would make him a trustworthy man of business. Whereunto he hath of late answered to the purport or effect following: 'You be d------d' or 'Go to Hell', or else when he hath been less under the influence of daffy, he has invited me in rather a dictatorial tone to 'Go and teach my granny to suck eggs!'*

But George had no ambitions yet to become a man of business. Unattached and with an accelerating reputation he was well known all over London, says George Augustus Sala, with his 'hawk nose, broad forehead, noticeable grey eyes, and black hair and whiskers ... blue swallow-tail coat, a buff waistcoat, grey pantaloons, and Hessian boots with tassels'. Nor, he added, was he 'averse from using his fists in an up-and-down tussle'.* Indeed, to judge from the many references to him in the gossip-sheets of the 1820s he was looked upon as a kind of 'Tom Spring with a turn for drawing – a bruising, gig-driving, badger-baiting, rat-matching, dog-and-duck-hunting pet of the Fancy'.*

The popular notion of George as an out-and-out hellraiser had in fact rather more currency than substance: he was immoderate in many things, impulsive, boisterous, and doubtless adventurous but the romances of his profligacy were the direct result of his connection with the immensely popular *Life in London*. This volume was what was fashionably known as a 'diorama' of London life, portrayed in a series of episodes in the lives of three flash young bucks dedicated to 'seeing life' no matter where they should chance upon it. The three heroes – Corinthian Tom, his rural cousin Jerry Hawthorn, and a truant scholar from Oxford by the name of Bob Logic – became instant cult-figures the moment the first instalments of the book were published in 1820, and their 'sprees' were aped, toasted, dramatised and enshrined in ballad and song all over London. The thirty-six illustrations were shared between George and his brother Robert, the text was by their old sporting acquaintance Pierce Egan.

W. T. Moncrieff, who later translated *Life in London* on to the stage, maintained that Tom, Jerry and Logic were modelled on George, Robert and Pierce Egan respectively: even the portraits in the book bore a striking resemblance to the three men in real life. And it was widely assumed that many of the adventures in the book were autobiographical – an impression that none of the authors seems to have done anything to dispel. This fact seems to have worried immensely William Bates,

Cruikshank's most ardent apologist, since he was forced to conclude that 'George, who was even then a moralist, either had misconceived the object of the author, or saw that his designs were used for a purpose he had not contemplated'!* Indeed, such was the wealth of detail, of places, characters and events (all easily identifiable by many of their readers) that much of it must have been first-hand. Under the pretext of introducing his country cousin into London society, Corinthian Tom takes us on a whirlwind tour of all the fashionable spots: Covent Garden, not to watch the performance but to inspect the parade of Cyprians (superior ladies of easy virtue) with their plumped-up breasts and rented finery; a subscription ball at Almack's where the social scrutiny was most exacting; the music and orchestras in Vauxhall Gardens, a masquerade supper at the Opera House, an assembly of 'heavy-heeled harlequins and orange-girls more inviting than their fruit'. (George once attended the masquerade in the costume of a dustman: so revolting was his make-up and convincing the realism with which he played his part that he was on the point of being thrown out. Only the arrival of his brother, splendidly attired as a cavalier, prevented an ugly scene.) And of course the more manly pastimes – a few rounds with Gentleman Jackson at his boxing academy in Bond Street, a morning at O'Shaunessy's fencing-rooms in St James's, a stroll round the bloodstock ring at Tattersall's, and a pipe with Egan's old friend Tom Cribb, the prize-fighting champion of all England.

In counterpoint to these glimpses of High Life we are also introduced to the seamier side of London (and incidentally of our heroes' characters). No end of a lark was had slumming it at a sluicery, or gin-shop, along with the derelicts and down-and-outs, then being hauled up before the beak at Bow Street for a breach of the peace. We meet, down at the docks, Flashy Nance the whore who could drink a sailor under the table, and Dirty Suke at Tothill Fields whose tears could not roll down her cheeks for the dirt; we watch Maccacco the marvel-monkey tearing dogs to pieces down at Westminster Pit, we pause to applaud the histrionic contortions of the beggars in the Holy Land, inspect the wretched tide of humanity flowing in and out of the whistling-shop (the pawnbroker's) and observe the condemned men hustled off to execution in Newgate. All this punctuated, for our dashing trio, by street-brawls, drinking-bouts and the finest sport of all – tormenting the Charleys, the parish watchmen, by overturning their sentry-boxes and leaving the occupant pinned-down and helpless.

No sooner was *Life in London* on the bookstalls than there was an epidemic of Charley-baiting all over the city. 'Even in so quiet a neighbourhood as Kennington then was,' Vizetelly noted, 'the watchman's box posted at the corner of a narrow turning facing the common was on several occasions toppled over on its slumbering inmate, by parties of young bloods fresh from flowing bowls of punch at the neighbouring Vauxhall Gardens.' (Another eight years were to pass before Robert Peel's policemen appeared in the streets.) Whatever else, *Life in London* captured the self-seeking spirit of the times and its success was phenomenal. The 'Corinthian' style in hats and boots became all the rage, the faces of Tom and Jerry adorned countless articles of pottery, teaboards and advertisements, their songs set to music with a score of tunes. They became synonyms of their age and, said Surtees a generation later, 'had a great deal to answer for in the way of leading soft-headed young men astray'. Their exploits were translated into French, pirated in America, and were dramatised in five different London theatres at the same time – as well as being metamorphosed somehow or other into an 'equestrian drama' for Davies' Royal Amphitheatre.

These dramatisations seem to have been based more closely on George and Robert's characterisations than on Egan's somewhat esoteric text. Indeed, Vizetelly remarked, 'Moncrieff had a contemptible opinion of Pierce Egan's share in the performance from the very outset, for years afterwards I heard him tell my father that when he dramatised the work he pitched the letterpress into the fire, and wrote the play from the etchings alone, remarking that he had often nettled Pierce Egan by telling him the same thing'. It was an academic point anyway, since none of the authors gained much except notoriety from these by-products of their book. Egan quite possibly may have proposed an early sequel to the two brothers without any success, since George went to the trouble to etch a print 'for Pierce Egan' in which Tom and Jerry have been brought to an untimely end (which was reportedly how George had envisaged the denouement to *Life in London* in the first place). The etching, 'The Tears of Pierce Egan for the Death of *Life in London*', portrays the funeral of Tom and Jerry attended by mourners from all their adventures – Bob Logic, Corinthian Kate, prize-fighters, fish-women, and Charleys – who, needless to say, are beside themselves with joy. In fact Tom and Jerry didn't die. In 1830 Egan composed a sequel, *Finish to the Adventures of Tom, Jerry and Logic*, but without the services of George, Robert providing all the illustrations. In this version Corinthian Tom gets his deserts, by breaking his neck in the hunting-field. Jerry Hawthorn however is permitted to return home and marry his childhood sweetheart, Mary Rosebud.

For all that, George did not entirely desert the genre. In 1822 an imitation (one of many) appeared, entitled *Life in Paris*, which purported to show the progress of another Corinthian, Dick Wildfire, and his cronies through the French capital. Curiously all the plates are by George, who had never so much as set foot outside his native land (nor, indeed, was he ever known to venture further afield than a day trip to Boulogne in his entire life). Maybe he was attracted by the sheer chauvinistic bias of the text – where in every encounter with the French our Corinthian comes off best –

but it was not a memorable book: in old age George could never recall who had written it although, says Jerrold, 'the man's name was always on the tip of his tongue'.* Of his better-travelled elder brother's influence there is no trace.

With *Life in London* George's close working association with Robert was already coming to an end. In 1818 Robert had got married and shortly afterwards moved into a house in King Street, deeper in the heart of the West End: meanwhile his mother decided to give up Dorset Street and took Eliza to live with her in Claremont Square, in the expanding but still partly rural suburb of Islington – where George joined them for a short time. Robert's ambition was now to set up in business as a watercolour and miniature painter, a calling of more social distinction (and one for which he had a marked talent), but one requiring a regular supply of rich patrons. These were not always as obligingly forthcoming as he might have hoped, and he was never able entirely to relinquish his illustrating and etching. He did acquire in due course a fashionable address in St James's Place, where by all accounts the hospitality was liberal and civilised: yet he never truly fulfilled the promise of his younger days.

There was much in Robert's work that was reminiscent of George's: not only were their subjects frequently the same, but at his best he was capable of a precision of detail and finish that could match his brother's. Too often, though, and especially in his etching, his work lacked the conscientiousness which (according to his friend George Daniel) he invariably applied to his watercolour drawings. Unlike his brother he came to regard his illustrations as hack work, and it would infuriate George – when his reputation was at its height – that publishers would deliberately advertise Robert's work as simply by 'Cruikshank'. One particular title, called just *Cruikshank at Home*, almost brought the two brothers to blows. When a third volume appeared, still without any acknowledgement that it was the work of Robert, not George, the younger man determined to air his grievance by publishing a sketch of himself removing the errant publisher, Kidd, by the nose with a pair of tongs, adding the request in a caption that 'His Friends and Public will observe that he has not any connexion with the works put forth by Mr Kidd of Chandos Street . . . nor ever intends to have'. The title of the fourth volume was duly changed, as the publisher drily announced, 'in consequence of the late disagreement between the two brothers Cruikshank (in reference to the question Which is the real Simon Pure?)'. This statement caused the curious entry in one edition of the German *Kunstler's Lexicon*: 'Pure (Simon), the real name of the celebrated caricaturist George Cruikshank'!

At least Robert knew which direction he wanted to take. George, with a dozen years or more of continuous work behind him, had achieved a measure of recognition, yet seemed perfectly content to exist on a purely hand-to-mouth level. John Gibson Lockhart, an eminent art critic of the day, succinctly summed up George's circumstances at this stage in his career. He wrote in an issue of *Blackwood's Magazine*

> It is high time that George Cruikshank should begin to think more than he seems to have hitherto of himself. Generally speaking, people consider him as a clever, sharp caricaturist and nothing more – a free-handed comical young fellow, who will do anything he is paid for, and who is quite contented to dine off the proceeds of a 'George IV' today and those of a 'Hone' or a 'Cobbett' tomorrow. He himself, indeed, appears to be the most careless creature alive, as touching his reputation. He seems to have no plan – almost no ambition – and, I apprehend, not much industry. He does just what is suggested or thrown in his way – pockets the cash, and orders his beef-steak and bowl . . . .*

Cruikshank, he implies, is at a watershed in his career and he goes on to offer him some well-meaning advice (which we shall be concerned with later on). But the message comes through loud and clear: if George is to develop as an artist he must settle down. Lockhart's proposed routine was anything but strenuous – including breakfast at nine-thirty, followed by a mere four hours of etching or painting, and the rest of the day devoted to mind-broadening activities. Such a schedule, George might have pointed out, might have suited an Academician: a self-employed etcher would have starved within weeks. All the same, whether by design or coincidence, the critic had made an opportune observation. George too thought it was time he 'settled down'.

George Cruikshank married Mary Walker, probably in 1823 or shortly after, and took her to live at 22 Amwell Street, just down the road from his mother's house in Claremont Square. He had turned thirty and she was sixteen or seventeen. In 1821, the date recently suggested for George's first marriage, Mary Walker was barely fourteen (as her death certificate shows). He might of course have taken the house (built in 1821) some time before the wedding. Mary is something of a mystery. There is no reason to suppose their marriage, lasting over twenty-five years, was anything but a compatible one, yet there is almost no reference to her in any of George's surviving letters or writings. Nor is she mentioned directly in any article or biographical essay published during George's lifetime or on his death: Blanchard Jerrold, of all people, virtually ignores her existence. It is indeed almost as if her husband deliberately destroyed all reference to his first wife before marrying again in 1850, as one leading Cruikshank collector has suggested.*

His motives for doing so can only be a matter for speculation, but we do know she presided over the not infrequent dinner-parties at Amwell Street with graciousness; Charles Dickens wrote affectionately of her, calling her George's 'stout lady'* (presumably in the sense of stout-hearted), and she often accompanied them on their excursions to the theatre. She produced no children, which must have been a disappointment to her paternally minded husband, but she did succeed in imposing some sort of domestic routine on the unpredictable pattern of his behaviour. Breakfast was always at eight, dinner at three, supper at nine in the evening: there was open house for callers between four and six – any other time they would find him incommunicado in his studio. Such orderliness came to suit George, who liked his homely comforts, his brandy-and-water after dinner in front of a roaring fire, for instance, enveloped by clouds of smoke from his long clay pipe. Where his wife was less successful was in curbing his all-male sorties on the town, after which he would invariably arrive home the worse for drink – but she did not tolerate them: when George knew he was too far gone, he preferred to stay out all night rather than face Mary.

At that time, according to Leigh's map of London (1827), the section of Amwell Street where the Cruikshanks lived was also known as Myddleton Terrace – which was the address George preferred to give on his published works. One such 'terrace' still survives in Amwell Street, though 22 has, sadly, been demolished. It was one of the brand-new, four-storey residences for the middle classes that were rapidly splicing semi-rural Islington with the teeming pavements of Clerkenwell and the city. When George moved there cows grazed beyond the back window, and you could walk across a field to Sadlers Wells: yet within five or six years the developers had triumphed, Myddleton Terrace had become a Square and St Mark's church was rising on the cow-pasture. It was still a pleasant and popular neighbourhood. Thomas Dibdin the impresario lived in the same row (George illustrated an edition of his father's famous songs), as did Edward Irving the Scottish mystic, whose 'voices' warned him of a Second Coming and got him into trouble with his church. Islington itself had a distinctive cultural life: Charles and Mary Lamb entertained at Colebrooke Cottage, Robert Seymour, the talented and tragic caricaturist, lived and died just the other side of the Angel. The greatest of all clowns, Joseph Grimaldi, lived just off the Hill and was president of a select little club at the Sir Hugh Myddleton public house, called the Crib, which counted George amongst its members. Sadlers Wells theatre, if not at the height of its reputation, offered a wide variety of diversions from pantomime to aquatic spectacles, and the White Conduit House (site of Thomas Lord's earliest cricket pitch) with its shrimps and ale was a favourite Sunday rendezvous for Cockneys trooping up past George's front window.

For the best part of thirty years – in 1834 he took on the lease of 23 next door as well – George was to be a familiar figure in these streets and gardens and ale-houses, observing with those 'steely blue eyes that struck through you ... peering through clouds of tobacco smoke and over foaming tankards in all kinds of strange and queer places',* sometimes pausing to jot down some curious feature on anything to hand, a thumbnail or one of his disposable false cuffs – which, rumour had it, provided his laundry-woman with a small unofficial income. A portrait of George in this period of his life, by the Irish artist Daniel Maclise, appeared in *Fraser's Magazine*: it displayed him in a pot-house, seated cross-legged on a barrel of beer, his tankard and pipe by him, sketching some scene on the crown of his hat. Not yet noticeably old-fashioned in his dress (it became his boast that he was the last person in London to keep wearing Hessian boots), he looks almost raffish as if occupied on some Tom-and-Jerry escapade. The keen, penetrating gaze is almost disconcerting.*

Maclise's portrait was frequently reproduced, and was a source of great embarrassment to George in his later temperance days: it was a figment of Maclise's imagination, who had not even met him at that date, he complained. He did not make sketches in ale-houses, he said, although he did admit to 'studying and observing nature' for the characters he then set before the public.* According to the article that accompanied the portrait in *Fraser's* – written by the captious journalist Maginn – George was in fact 'shocked at the evil fate which consigns him to drawing sketches and caricatures, instead of letting him loose in his natural domain of epic or historical picture'. That is to be doubted, except in so far as George *did* nurture ambitions to be a painter, but these were as much the offspring of ill-considered advice from others as of his own yearnings for the higher reaches of art.

William Maginn was a close friend of Lockhart, and would certainly have known of his profile of Cruikshank in *Blackwood*'s in which, as we have already seen, George was advised to take stock of his career and position in life. In that piece Lockhart had rashly suggested George was capable of 'designing as many Annunciations, Beatifications, Apotheoses, Metamorphoses and so forth as would cover York Cathedral from end to end. It is still more impossible to doubt that he might be a famous portrait painter'. Further on he returns to his theme: 'Seriously, Cruikshank must attend to the hint we have been giving him, and learn to respect himself. He must give up his mere slang drudgery, and labour to be what nature has put within his reach – not a caricaturist but a painter.'

It is hard to say precisely what effect Lockhart's critique had upon George: certainly he did not instantly turn to painting – he hadn't properly acquired the training or technique for it, and was never to do so. Yet the *Blackwood*'s article represented a milestone in his career. There had been praise and popularity before, but this was the first serious assessment of George's talent as an *artist* by a recognised authority in a respected journal – and it was unstinting in its praise. To dip into it almost at random:

> . . . a fact it undoubtedly is that he possesses genius – genius in its truest sense – strong, original English genius. Look round the world of art and ask, how many are there of whom anything like this can be said? Why, there are not half a dozen names that could bear being mentioned at all; and certainly there is not one, the pretensions of which will endure sifting, more securely and more triumphantly than that of George Cruikshank.

Very gratifying stuff, but also calculated to raise a few niggling doubts in the artist's mind about the application of his approved talent. 'Cruikshank may, if he pleases, be a second Gillray,' Lockhart had said, 'but this should not be his ambition. He is fitted for a higher walk.'

It is misleading to suggest – as it has been suggested – that George abandoned political and personal satire after 1823, when the *Blackwood*'s article was published. He continued to supply the print-shops for several years with some excellent plates, though more spasmodically, and often from designs made by his friends Alfred Forrester ('Crowquill'), William Merle ('Bird') and Frederick Marryat, who found relaxation from his romances of the high seas in penning gentle naval caricatures. Compared with the halcyon years of Napoleon or Caroline, Cruikshank's output is certainly sparse, but this must be seen against the political background of the 1820s. Until the death of Lord Liverpool in 1827 and the agitation for Catholic emancipation that plagued successive governments, the political scene was moribund for the cartoonists: print-sellers were offering only a handful of political prints from any source. Good old-fashioned controversy was flagging, and only the boom in Reform satires of the early 1830s gave the print-shops a temporary respite in their declining fortunes.

In this vacuum George naturally sought other occupation. It so happened that Lockhart had written his generous article in *Blackwood*'s on the publication of Part I of a small volume called *Points of Humour* (1823), a collection of humorous fables, poems and anecdotes each one illustrated by an etching and woodcuts from George, not an entirely new departure, as four years earlier he had contributed some coloured etchings to a series called *The Humourist* (an anthology of 'Witty Sayings, Bon Mots and Jeux d'Esprits'). 'It was for the purpose of puffing it and its author, and of calling upon all who have eyes to water and sides to ache to buy it, that I began this leading lecture,' he explained. And buy it they did: these little masterpieces of comic illustration instantly caught the public fancy. The first edition was exhausted almost on publication, and one reviewer raved: 'In this little volume of little plates he has established his reputation as a great master . . . these pointed emanations of his prolific point are unique gems of humour.'* In fact George's *Points of Humour* represent a midway stage between his satires and his book-plates. They are not caricatures exactly, nor are they dramatic representations. They are burlesques, self-contained little situation-comedies: the ponderous procession of clerics tumbling *en masse* down the steps, the cuckolding squire finding his kidnapped breeches 'advertised' by the town-crier, the 'coward' stampeding his brother-officers by lighting a grenade in the mess.

The book is in reality a vehicle for Cruikshank's illustrations (some editions were published without the text), and its success made it the prototype for similar ventures with the same publisher, Charles Baldwyn. The following year he brought out *Italian Tales of Humour, Gallantry and Romance*, which contained one of George's 'suppressed' plates. The illustration in question, entitled 'The Dead Rider', shows a monk caught short and, in frustration at the slowness of its occupant, hurling stones at the door of the privy: unknown to him but not to the reader the offending monk inside is dead. This plate – scarcely one to have given offence to an eighteenth-century audience – was replaced in the second edition, sure testimony to a refining of public taste that was shortly to become 'Victorian'. Hot on the heels of *Italian Tales* came a selection of humorous court-reports culled from the columns of the *Morning Herald* entitled *Mornings at Bow Street*. Both volumes contain the same delicate, animated vignettes – some no more than $2\frac{1}{2}$ inches square embrace a dozen or more figures – and as in *Points of Humour* the most important ingredient is obviously Cruikshank, a role which George came to expect and which later brought him into direct confrontation with less self-effacing authors.

From 1823 and his significant but brief association with Baldwyn (whose daughter, Eliza, became George's second wife a quarter of a century later) dates Cruikshank's whole-hearted commitment to books. He was discovering that not only could they inspire serious critical acclaim but, more prosaically, they offered the prospect of substantial employment. The English book trade in the second quarter of the nineteenth century underwent a remarkable period of expansion: by 1850 publishers were offering more than 2,500 new titles a year, as compared with an annual average in the first quarter of about 500. It was George's good fortune that his rare talents were available and recognised at the very beginning of this explosion: and by the same token it is also true his own popularity and soaring imgination helped to assure the commercial success of an astonishing range of titles during this eventful period.

To Baldwyn George was indebted for one particularly happy commission, which was to reveal one of the most enduring aspects of his genius. For several years the folklore studies of the Grimm brothers had been exciting interest in Germany, and in 1822 the final volume of their *Fairy Tales* had been published in German. The following year Baldwyn obtained a selection of them translated into English by John Edward Taylor, and passed them to George for illustration, so unearthing a rich new vein of fantastical humour. In their way, his etchings for *German Popular Stories* (1823) were as influential as the Grimms' original work on oral tradition: they fixed the fauna and topography of fairyland for generations to come. For the rest of his life – and he returned frequently to this magic world – George towered, like one of his own shaggy giants, over the landscape of enchanted forests, mysterious castles, mischievous imps and frolicsome witches. It was, as Thackeray maintained, as if he had been amongst them '. . . and brought back their portraits in his sketch-book. He alone is the only designer fairy-land has had, alone has had a true insight into the character of the "little people". They are something like men and women, and yet not flesh and blood; they are laughing and mischievous but we know not why. Mr Cruikshank, however, has had some dream or the other . . . or else some preternatural fairy revelation, which has made him acquainted with the looks and ways of the fantastical subjects of Oberon and Titania.'* The appeal of these diminutive etchings percolated back into Germany, where they were published with great approval, and nearly half a century later they were reissued in England to accompany a new edition of Grimm, where Ruskin in his preface likened them to the best of Rembrandt.

The supernatural, so beloved of the Romantics with their Gothic fantasies and apocalyptic visions, was given a much more genial face in Cruikshank's hands. He did not have the brooding, diabolic nature of a Fuseli (who was reputed to nourish his nightmares by consuming raw meat before retiring): when George's chairs and tables are moved by some extra-terrestial force they dance and chuckle, his hobgoblins are merry little souls. Even where he was called on to explore the darker reaches of the supernatural, as in his designs for von Chamisso's *Peter Schlemihl* (1823), they turn out eerie rather than downright sinister. This classic of German romanticism, with its echoes of Faust, tells the story of the man who sold his shadow to the devil in return for a bottomless purse, only to discover he has bartered away his peace of mind too. The etchings in which the devil gleefully rolls up the shadow like a piece of black velvet, and where shadowless Peter sits, haunted, amid the candlelit shadows, have deep pathos but no passion. Nonetheless, when these too were republished in Germany Chamisso declared himself quite delighted by them.

Baldwyn's advertisements show that all his ventures with Cruikshank sold remarkably well, running to two or sometimes three editions within a few months, and it was not long before other publishers were beating a path to George's door with anthologies of humorous and curious tales, which were clearly regarded as the artist's special domain. The publisher James Robins, of Ivy Lane, appears to have had an almost inexhaustible supply. Over the next four years he published Cruikshank's illustrations to *Tales of Irish Life* (1824), *Memoirs of Lord Byron* (published in parts 1824/5), which were actually illustrations to his writings, *Greenwich Hospital* (1826), a 'series of naval sketches by an Old Sailor', *More Mornings at Bow Street* (1827), and *Eccentric Tales* (1827), translations from the German of von Kosewitz's stories. The striking thing was how often Cruikshank's publishers chose to issue portfolio editions of the plates on their own, without a word of text and sometimes charging as much as for the original edition. This must have struck George as well. Why, he must have pondered over his late-night brandies, did they need the letterpress in the first place? On his reputation a book of pure illustrations was clearly a sound commercial proposition. Logic prompted a further consideration: why did he need a publisher either? Without him George would be free to follow his own fancies.

In the summer of 1826 George made up his mind: he would indeed be his own publisher. His first enterprise appeared in August, *Phrenological Illustrations* ('Published by George Cruikshank, Myddleton Terrace, Pentonville'), six large plates each with several designs, bound together in a yellow wrapper was sold for 8s. plain, 12s. coloured. It was a fruitful and timely topic to choose – opinions on the fashionable 'science' of phrenology were rupturing the medical world. The craniological system of Dr Franz Gall, who argued that human characteristics were related to the shape of the skull and that each of our attributes has a designated place within the brain, had long been banned in Vienna, its birthplace. The apostles of Dr Gall however had continued to spread the word, and Gall himself had made a lecture tour of England in 1823, not very successfully. Since then, though, two English treatises on phrenology, by Combe and de Ville, had generated a great deal of heat, if not much light, on the subject and de Ville's phrenology clinic in the Strand was doing good business.

What fascinated George, as a student of human nature, were some of the curious human characteristics Gall claimed to have isolated in the cranium – philoprogenitiveness, amativeness, inhabitiveness, adhesiveness, to mention but a few. Why, it opened up all sorts of possibilities for struggling artists who had previously had to content themselves with such commonplace emotions like love, grief or fear. George's analysis, for instance, of philoprogenitiveness – literally, an inclination to produce offspring – produced a *ménage* of gushing, long-nosed children besieging an equally long-nosed, gushing father. This was the plate which Thackeray, as a member of a schoolboy syndicate formed to purchase *Phrenological Illustrations*, had the good fortune to win in the share-out and which he long treasured:

> The artist has at the back of his own skull, we are certain, a huge bump of philoprogenitiveness [he wrote later]. He loves children in his heart; every one of those he has drawn is perfectly happy and jovial, and affectionate, and innocent as possible. He makes them with large noses, but he loves them, and you always find something kind in the midst of his humour, and the ugliness redeemed by a sly touch of beauty. The smiling mother reconciles one with all the hideous family; they have something of the mother in them – something kind, and generous and tender.*

The response to this slim volume cannot have disappointed George, for the following May he published *Illustrations of Time* in exactly the same format, with the promise of another six prints 'on the same subject as the present work at the latter end of the year'. These punning little sketches on the theme of time (Time Was, Killing Time, Pastime . . . &c.) are exquisitely etched, and were still being reissued more than twenty-five years later.

The artistic independence gained by his own publications certainly relieved George of what, at times, he came to think of as the tyranny of publishers – his long career was punctuated by a series of feuds with one or other of them. He continued to publish some of his work from Myddleton Terrace until 1835, but it was not without its problems. That George was no business man was soon obvious from the dispute with *Bell's Life in London*. This journal had first seen the light of day in 1824 as *Pierce Egan's Life in London* (to which George had contributed a few sporting woodcuts – and an advertisement for Wycombe Sauce!), but had been merged with *Bell's Life* in 1827, when Egan had profitably sold out.

What appears to have happened is that the editor of the new newspaper, a friend of George's by name of Dowling, approached the artist for permission to reproduce some of the *Phrenological Illustrations* and *Illustrations of Time*. In granting this permission George failed to take the elementary precaution of stipulating which sketches might be used, and when the paper was published discovered to his horror that the editor had assumed he had *carte blanche* and had appropriated nearly all of them under the heading 'Gallery of Comicalities' (which became a regular feature of the paper and later boasted such artists as Leech and Meadows). To make matters worse, these Comicalities were afterwards published separately, in direct competition with George's own books. Seeking an injunction to stop such flagrant piracy he was privately warned against the cost of the necessary litigation, and reluctantly retired from the lists without recovering a penny.

Publishers were not always without their uses. George never felt the pinch of outright poverty, but financial crises and temporary embarrassments were almost a part of his way of life. 'No one has worked harder than I have,' he once confessed, 'but my fate seems to be just like that old gentleman who was compelled to roll a stone up a hill – and when it got to the top, down rolled the stone again.'* No sooner had George rolled his stone to the top than something – a pressing creditor, household expenses, importunate friends or relatives – toppled it down again. 'My motto was "At it again", and up I rolled the lump again.' At such moments George would unashamedly plead his plight with one of his publishers: in due course he became a master at these distress letters, which he would embellish with bright little jokes and quaint doodled sketches. His appeal to James Robins, while he was working on the sketches for *Greenwich Hospital*, was characteristically breezy:

> I am sorry to find you will be 'poor this week'. I have been so this some time
> – but really joking apart I have promised to pay about 8 pounds this week
> which I must do by hook or by crook. Try what you can do for me. You
> will find that after another week or so my requests will be exceedingly
> moderate. You of course see that I am working hard. . . . I wish you wd
> give me a bit of blotting paper.*

His close friends often testified to George's open-handedness (when he had the money) to anyone in need: equally he could harbour a stubborn resentment against anyone whom he considered had short-changed him for his work, and no one suffered more from George's intransigence than his old friend, William Hone.

Since 1822, George had worked little for Hone, whose list had taken on a decidedly scholarly tone, but their 'mutual esteem' (according to the publisher)* remained undiminished; and when in 1826 Hone launched a weekly periodical, *The Every-Day Book*, George gladly contributed a number of woodcuts. Their relations were as cordial as ever the following year when Hone proposed an omnibus edition of their celebrated pamphlets, and the artist set his seal of approval on the project with a fraternal vignette on the title-page, showing the pair of them seated at a table in earnest collaboration. But even as it was being published Hone's financial affairs were in chaos – largely through the incompetence, or systematic fraud, of the accountant he employed to manage the business. Money that was owed to George never materialised, a bitter quarrel broke out – doubtless made the more irreconcilable by their very intimacy. For the next fifteen years, in spite of Hone's bankruptcy and imprisonment for debt, George refused even to speak to his former friend – though this may have been the result, less of his own inclinations, than of Mary Cruikshank's known suspicions of the publisher's 'horrid' unmarried daughters. (Even these strictures were overcome, when George received a plea from Mrs Hone to visit her husband's death-bed. The artist found the reconciliation so moving he vowed never to suffer a life-long estrangement from anyone ever again, and wept openly all the way to Hone's funeral – according to Dickens who accompanied him.)

Towards the end of June 1830 George IV died, commending his subjects for their good taste in praying for his recovery, but in truth barely remembered and scarcely mourned. In his last years he had visited London but rarely, the capital he wanted so much to make the most beautiful in the world but which had repaid him with catcalls and derision. But in his absence London had been developing in its own way and with gathering momentum. The world of *Life in London* (1820) had still been essentially one of eighteenth-century values and social organisations, of duelling and dandies, mobs and anarchy, high life and low life. The London of Cruikshank's *Scraps and Sketches* (1828–32) is a city in transition, gradually succumbing to the subterranean rumblings of reform, to the pressures of population and technology, and to the 'improvements' of middle-class materialism.

The four parts of *Scraps and Sketches* demonstrate most clearly the benefits of artistic freedom on George. His pencil wanders at will between satire and social comment, whimsy and farce, capturing the fancies of the moment. The feminine fashions in 'A Scene in Kensington Gardens' are as outrageous as ever, even daring with their tantalising glimpse of ankle, but the lethargic gentlemen – prototypes of the later 'dundrearies' – have already adopted the grey uniformity of Victorian taste. Among the working class the urge to 'betterment' is now apparent: the chimney-sweep in 'Gentility' refuses to take part in the sweeps' traditional May-day rout on account of that being 'Werry low', and is going out to dinner instead. In 'The Grand March of Intellect' the massed ranks of infant clerks bear witness to the popularity of the new mechanics' institutes and Brougham's Society for the Diffusion of Useful Knowledge, founded in 1827.

With the population pressing on one and a half million, architects no longer talked of confining London within prescribed boundaries, and an era of untramelled suburban development was under way. In 'London Going out of Town' George protests at the rape of the countryside in general, and that of Hampstead in particular, where copyholders were fighting a rearguard action against enclosure; cohorts of bricklayer's hod-like automatons advance against the hayricks and grazing flocks, to extend the limits of their jerry-built empire. But progress was inevitable, and one of its most bizarre manifestations was the steam-coach, celebrated by George in 'The Horses going to the Dogs': in December 1827 Mr Gurney's New Steam Carriage had paraded around Regent's Park at a stately five miles an hour, belching smoke and smelling (according to one eye-witness) of 'boiled iron'. Fortunately for the environment it never caught on, but the new-fangled omnibuses did (even if desperately uncomfortable for the corpulent passengers in 'Just Room for Three Insides'). The first of these trunk-like horse-drawn vehicles started service between Paddington and the Bank of England in July 1829, the overture to a transport revolution in London.

The agitation for parliamentary reform that exploded once again in the early 1830s was anticipated in the London of the twenties by less vociferous but equally dedicated movements for reform of the city's archaic administration. Parishes were run independently and often corruptly by 'select vestries', which in practice meant an unholy alliance of clergy and powerful parishioners as personified in 'Church and State', which self-perpetuating committees were responsible for the appointment of all parish officers, Vestry Clerks, Guardians of the Poor, Beadles and others. In 1826 St Paul's, Covent Garden, won the right to a democratic vestry, and in the next few years several other central parishes followed suit.

But the most telling blow to the authority of the vestries was Sir Robert Peel's formation of a Metropolitan Police Force in 1829, which swept away the ramshackle edifice of unpaid parish constables and bucolic watchmen. George hailed their arrival on the beat with 'The New Police "Act"', their first act therein being to apprehend the venal watchmen themselves with their pathetic rattles and lanterns. Within a few years the new police with their specially strengthened top-hats had cleared the streets of their marauding bands of desperadoes, and made it possible to cross a public park at night without waiting for sufficient travellers to gather together for protection.

Nevertheless, the social conditions persisted that bred crime and gave rise to spontaneous eruptions of violence, as at Smithfield's annual St Bartholomew's Fair which George well and truly grilled in 'The Devil's Frying Pan'. When its reputation got so bad that all exhibitions were banned in 1840, George persuaded himself that this purse-lipped print had finally stirred the authorities to action. But above all it was drink that remained the besetting vice, the more so since spirit duty had been reduced in 1825. Gin-shops had proliferated, and gaudy and glittering 'gin-palaces' had opened, strategically sited in poorer areas – a far cry from the verminous All-Max where Tom and Jerry had had their spree.

'The Gin Shop' is the most powerful of George's plates in *Scraps and Sketches*. Full of punning allegory, like the loaded gin-trap and the prancing spirits, it portrays a tattered family (including the babe-in-arms) drowning itself in gin, seduced by the spurious glamour of the marbled surroundings and wasp-waisted barmaid. Death stalks through the whole picture, in the demons, the coffins, the figure of Death himself disguised as a watchman. It seems, at first glance, as if George has begun his crusade against drink long before his days of water-drinking and fanatical teetotalism. But in fact the morality of 'The Gin Shop' is different from that of his later tracts, which set out to show that drink was the root cause of all crime and wickedness: this print is specifically an attack on the gin-palaces for the exploitation of the poor. Indeed, a few plates further on, George leaves us in no doubt of drink's respectable place in a decent fellow's scheme of things: in 'The Comfortables', an idyll of nineteenth-century homeliness, the farmer has his jug of ale, the bachelor his nightcap by the fire, the gourmet his array of decanters. They are all patently at peace with the world.

5 The Facts of Fiction
(1830-1842)

In November 1830 Peel's new policemen faced their first big test. The London mob, fired as ever by its own internal combustion, once again took to the streets baying after Reform. The hopes rekindled by the death of George IV and the arrival of the bluff, approachable 'Sailor King' had been quickened a month later by news from Paris, that a successful revolution had deposed the reactionary Charles X in favour of a 'citizen' King. The Opposition had gained more seats in the General Election in August and now, in November, the Tory ministry was on the verge of disintegration. The political omens were good but, as in 1819, it was economic forces that provoked action: the night skies to the south of London glowed regularly with the light of burning hayricks – the work (so the wall-slogans proclaimed) of the ubiquitous Captain Swing, but self-evidently the last desperate resort of unemployed farm-workers. In London the starving weavers of Spitalfields found the gates of Temple Bar closed against them, surged into the Strand only to be confronted by the solid ranks of Peelers. Time and again over the next eighteen months, as the Reform Bill floundered in and out of Parliament, the police were called out to do battle with the rioters: at times it was hard to tell if the rallying cry was 'The Bill, the whole Bill and nothing but the Bill,' or 'Away with the Police'. There were countless broken heads, and nothing would deny the demonstrators their time-honoured custom of smashing all the windows of opponents of reform (notably the Duke of Wellington's), but unlike other cities London emerged largely unscathed from the Reform disturbances. In Bristol the city centre was fired by rioters and destroyed.

Some of the old familiar radical faces, Cobbett and Carlile, re-emerged in those momentous months: others like Cruikshank, it was noted, held aloof. In February 1831 the reformist paper *The Ballot* remarked acidly: 'We have heard that George Cruikshank – and it occurs to us at this time to mention it – is on the pension list. He declines engraving or designing political caricatures and has done so since the days of Hone's celebrated pamphlets . . . this is a graver charge than that against Johnson.' Dr Johnson (in the days of Fox and Burke) *had* elected to become a government hack, but the injustice of this implication obviously stung George into retaliation. The next month, to prove he was nobody's Tory last-ditcher, he produced two Reform satires,

'The System that Works so Well' showing the House of Commons in an advanced state of decay, and 'Sweeping Measures' which depicted Lord John Russell with his new broom clearing the House of borough-mongerers.

So far as they went, George's satires purveyed solid Whig orthodoxy, but were scarcely radical. Only the die-hards any longer opposed the dismantling of the rotten boroughs, the worst of which Russell summed up as 'a ruined mound, three inches of stone wall, and a park without the vestige of a dwelling, each returning its two members to the Imperial Parliament'. On the far more controversial issue of universal suffrage George was mute, and prudently so for the sake of his reputation, if his views were those openly expressed during the second Reform Bill, and as set forth in the *British Bee-Hive* '. . . if "universal suffrage" were granted, if everything were allowed or even a great part of what is asked for, if *everyone* had a vote, it would cease to be a monarchy and would become a REPUBLIC'. It was not that George had lost his passion for a cause – indeed, in 1832 when an appalling epidemic of cholera swept through London he produced two trenchant attacks, on the inefficiency of the newly appointed boards of health, and in 'Salus Populi Suprema Lex' on the owner of Southwark Water Works who continued to supply thousands of homes with water drawn from the Thames at the very spot where the city's main sewers emptied into it.

The fact was, emancipation was no longer George's cause, nor politics in general a major preoccupation. By the age of forty George was an unmistakable ornament of London's literary and artistic establishment: his own intimate circle included the novelist Frederick Marryat, Thomas Tegg the publisher, the critic Gibson Lockhart, the artist Clarkson Stanfield, and the playwright Douglas Jerrold. And in due course he was inevitably drawn into the galaxies that orbited around Dickens, Harrison Ainsworth, their publisher Richard Bentley: at their tables he met and amused many other luminaries, the editor Leigh Hunt, Edward Bulwer-Lytton, the young Thackeray.

George was agreed to be good company at such gatherings, convivial and gregarious. 'Will you dine with us?' Dickens wrote to Ainsworth. 'The illustrious George and his stout lady are coming, so that the Anti-Bores will be triumphant and keep the Bores in due subjection.'* According to his son,* Thomas Tegg was so struck one evening by George's mirthfulness at table, and by the staid, unresponsive demeanour of his neighbour, that he mischievously suggested the two of them should collaborate on a book. In the event they did so, a collection of short stories by the pseudonymous Carlton Bruce, and called *Mirth and Morality* (1834). His after-dinner entertainments were widely celebrated – he could dance the hornpipe quite as well as the popular actor T. P. Cooke, and frequently did so. His repertoire of songs included

'The Loving Ballad of Lord Bateman', which he had been taught by a dustman called Brandy Tom in an ale-house, an occasion he later recalled in one of his 'posterity' plates and explained to Charles Hancock: 'I was out one evening for a stroll, having got to Maiden Lane, Battle Bridge. A great many dustmen lived in that quarter, and artists are obliged to mix and make friends with all sorts of people – I must admit that some of my friends at that time were not very select . . .'. George's rendering of 'Lord Bateman', with him mimicking the several characters in the saga, became a popular cabaret turn with his friends and in 1839 – probably at Dickens's instigation – he published the song with a set of interesting but uncharacteristic line-drawings. The introduction was written anonymously by Charles Dickens, who was very cross when he discovered his authorship had somehow been leaked to the *Morning Post*. Curiously, at exactly the same time, Thackeray heard the song and also conceived the idea of publishing it. He wrote to George in May 1839: 'I want to tell you of an event which need not much alarm you – I heard Dickens sing 'Lord Bateman', and went home straight and made a series of drawings to it: which are now in part on copper and sold to a publisher. Only two days ago I heard that you were occupied with the same subject. I'm not such a fool as to suppose that my plates can hurt yours: but warning is fair between friends and I hope thro' death and eternity we shall always be such.' There is no evidence that Thackeray's version was published, although in the London Library an 1870 edition of the song is ascribed to him.

'Cruikshank keeps his ground I see,' wrote the journalist Lamon Blanchard to Ainsworth.* 'May his tankard never be less, and his whiskers flourish a thousand years. Pray heaven he hath not lost his voice singing of anthems! When you see him give the least of his admirers – yet no little one either – a lift in his jolly remembrance.' But if George could be jolly for some, there were others who considered him mildly eccentric in society, with his long flowing mane, his penetrating gaze and peculiar mode of dress. James Grant in one of his Portraits of Public Characters observed:

> He is a very singular and, in some respects, eccentric man, considered, as what he himself would call, 'a social being'. The ludicrous and extraordinary fancies with which his mind is constantly teeming often impart a sort of wildness to his look, and peculiarity to his manner, which would suffice to frighten from his presence those unacquainted with him. He is often so uncourteous and abrupt in his manner as to incur the charge of seeming rude.*

George riposted to this charge in characteristic fashion – by penning a humorous sketch of an assembled company frightened out of their wits by his mere arrival in the room – adding a little plaintively that he was himself unconscious of his dire effect on folk. 'But enjoying this happy unconsciousness, sharing it moreover with my friends, why wake me from the delusion?' he remarked. 'Why excite my imagination, and unstring my nerves, with visions of nursery-maids flying before me in my suburban walks – of tender innocents in arms frightened into fits at my approach, of five-bottle men turning pale in my presence, of banquet-halls deserted on my entrance!'*

Abrupt he certainly could be, disconcerting even his close friends at times – but from impulsiveness rather than intentional churlishness. And even his wilder outbursts could be redeemed by his obviously ingenuous nature. Charles Dickens recalled one particularly riotous evening: 'George Cruikshank was perfectly wild at the reunion; and after singing all manner of maniac songs, wound up the entertainment by coming home (six miles) in a little open phæton of mine, *on his head* – to the mingled delight and indignation of the metropolitan police.'*

It was not, however, simply for his bonhomie that George was welcome at the dinner-table: he was ungrudgingly acknowledged to be the most popular illustrator of the day. By the end of the 1830s he could command £12 for a single plate, almost double the fee which younger artists like Hablot Browne (Phiz) or John Leech could hope to ask for at the time. Authors who secured George's services as illustrator could be almost embarrassing in their prefatory outpourings of gratitude. Thus William Clarke in the preface to his *Three Course and a Dessert*: '. . . [to George Cruikshank] he is deeply indebted for having embellished his rude sketches in their transfer to wood, and translated them into a proper pictorial state. They have necessarily acquired a value which they did not intrinsically possess, in passing through the hands of that distinguished artist.' Vizetelly was being slightly unfair when he claimed George's designs had been the means of saving the work from oblivion, but it is true that his parade of anthropomorphic ingredients – the highly supercilious mushroom, the contented oyster, the bacchanalian group of lemons – distinguished it from many another book of anecdotes.

As a book-illustrator George was in a unique, and sometimes anomalous, position. His status as an artist allowed him to arrange for a writer to 'write up' his sketches or at least work from his ideas (for example, *Sunday in London*, 1833) and, in rare instances, even become an equal contractual partner in a work of fiction, as was agreed for Ainsworth's *The Tower of London* (1840). Such a proposition, almost unthinkable in the latter half of the century, indicates that the new art of illustrating fiction was still close to its documentary origins in graphic satire. As often as not the print-makers of old had dreamed up the idea, written the captions, executed the design and etched it as well: and some early illustrated works of fiction were an extension of this (i.e. Rowlandson's *Dr Syntax* and, to some extent, *Life in London*). George was the one artist whose career spanned the whole of this transition period, and he was never able to reconcile himself entirely to a subordinate role. Without reference to this historical development, George's subsequent confrontations and controversies with authors seem like pure ego-mania, which they were not.

The fifteen years or so after 1830 were Cruikshank's most prosperous period, when his output was truly prodigious. Some of his designs were on wood – which since its revival by Thomas Bewick (*d.* 1828) had become a popular printing medium with publishers, since it offered far longer runs than either copper or steel plates – and the cutting of these was usually entrusted to one of a select band of professional engravers, Williams, Landells or Thompson, who was reputed to have kept a set of special tools, silver mounted with ivory handles, exclusively for work on George's designs, or later Vizetelly or the Dalziel brothers. But the early etchings were all done by George's hand, with only an assistant at Myddleton Terrace to help with biting-in. One of his assistants, Joseph Sleap, had been promoted from the kitchen to the studio and, under his master's guidance, showed flair enough for drawing to sell his own sketches. But Joseph's prime impediment was his habit of nodding off at any time of day, apparently under the influence of opium (which ultimately proved fatal). Charles Dickens was intrigued, on his visits to Pentonville, by Joe, who seemed to pass his days as in a dream – and eventually reincarnated him as Fat Boy in *The Pickwick Papers*.

The vogue for 'popular' editions of classic works – which reached its peak in the late forties – was already under way and providing George with his bread-and-butter money (and, it must be supposed, an excellent grounding in literature). For *Roscoe's Novelist's Library* (1831–33) he produced scores of plates for works by Smollett, Fielding, Goldsmith, Cervantes and Sterne, and dozens for Fisher's complete re-issue of the Waverley Novels (1836–38). In Major's edition of Defoe's *Robinson Crusoe* (1831) he could not resist, according to the publisher's own preface, endowing the hero with his own likeness which, however much of a landlocked sailor George might have fancied himself, was hardly a piece of self-flattery in view of the obvious shortage of razors on Crusoe's island.

More satisfying from the artist's point of view were those novels which now began to be issued in monthly serial form (as opposed to the former practice of issuing two or three volumes by subscription). This arrangement involved the illustrator in the creative stages of the novel, perhaps helping to 'visualise' the more dramatic episodes and – to George's way of thinking – realising his potential as 'the modern Hogarth'. *Life in London* had first been published in parts with great success, but since then nothing had generated the excitement and anticipation that greeted the continuing instalments of Charles Dickens's *The Pickwick Papers* in 1836, which a contemporary claimed eclipsed all interest in the politics of the day and found poverty-stricken admirers 'flattening their noses against the booksellers' windows . . . eager to peruse every line of the letterpress that might be exposed to view, frequently reading it aloud to applauding bystanders'.

Dickens was known to the public at that time only as Boz, and the author of some entertaining 'Sketches' that kept popping up in various periodicals. Towards the end of 1835, while Dickens was writing his final series of Sketches, the publisher John Macrone suggested a collected edition, to be illustrated by Cruikshank. In November, Dickens obtained 'a long interview' with the artist thereby 'gratifying my long cherished wish to obtain an introduction to a gentleman whose much appreciated talents (I don't say it egotistically) no one appreciates so highly as myself',* and arranged for George to start work on his plates at once. In their correspondence over the next two months Dickens clearly takes pains to show George the deference due to his reputation and the twenty years' difference in their ages – at the same time impatiently complaining to Macrone that George 'needed a spur applied', since he had only produced three plates in a fortnight. Almost immediately he retracted this charge of negligence, when it was discovered that each plate contained no less than four drawings, and with the book all but completed sent George in the first week of January a preview of his preface to *Sketches by Boz*. It was everything the artist could have hoped for from a young author appearing in hard-cover for the first time:

> Entertaining no inconsiderable feeling of trepidation, at the idea of making so perilous a voyage in so frail a machine, alone and unaccompanied, the author was naturally desirous to secure the assistance and companionship of some well-known individual, who had frequently contributed to the success, though his well-earned reputation rendered it impossible for him ever to have shared the hazard, of similar undertakings. To whom, as possessing this requisite in an eminent degree, could he apply but to GEORGE CRUIKSHANK?

For the 'enlarged' edition of *Boz*, which was published in June 1839, a few months after Dickens had rejected George's 'fireside plate' for *Oliver Twist*, George etched a frontispiece which was obviously a sly reminder to the author of these blandishments: it shows a crowd cheering Dickens's ascent in a hot-air balloon – his 'frail machine' – along with George – his 'assistant and companion'.

The world of Boz in this first series – of anonymous desk clerks in chop-houses eating their solitary suppers, of pawnbrokers and 4/6d. dancing academies, Sundays in the tea-gardens, fatuous beadles and unmarriageable maidens – was already familiar ground to George. He had observed and captured some of its idiosyncrasies in his own *Sketchbook* (1834–36), a medley of character-studies, curious physiognomies and humorous situations; indeed, these people had been his raw material all his life. So it was not at all displeasing for him to find that the reviewers had got their priorities right. 'Boz is the Cruikshank of writers,' proclaimed *The Spectator*.

When a second series of *Sketches by Boz* was proposed in the autumn of 1836, George made up his mind that this would be much more of a collaborative effort than the first series had been – only to discover that Macrone had set the whole of Dickens's text up in type before consulting George. Piqued, he wrote to the publisher that he had another commission to finish before he could even start on the second volume of Boz, and went on: 'I did expect to see that MS. from time to time in order that I might have the privilege of suggesting any little alterations to suit the Pencil, but if you are printing the book all that sort of thing is out of the question. Only this much I must say, that unless I can get good subjects to work upon, I will not work at all.'*

This infuriated Dickens when he got to hear about it. 'I have long believed Cruikshank to be mad; and his letter therefore surprises me not a jot,' he wrote back to Macrone.* Crossly he suggested he tell the artist '*from me* that I am very much amused at the notion of his altering my manuscript, and that had it fallen into his hands, I should have preserved his emendations as "curiosities of Literature". Most decidedly am I of the opinion that he may just go to the Devil . . . .' It may be assumed that Macrone did not pass this message on and that the contretemps was tactfully smoothed over, since ten days later Dickens was inviting the Cruikshanks to a performance of his play, *The Strange Gentleman*, at the St James's Theatre (which George frankly informed the author had been very badly acted).

On a personal level their friendship blossomed, the two men drawn together by their clubbable natures and passion for the theatre. George became an active member of Dickens's amateur theatrical group, which performed in London in the 1840s and once went on a long tour of the provinces (his performances as Pistol in *The Merry Wives of Windsor* and in other, now-forgotten pieces were, by all accounts, somewhat over-coloured). And very likely it was George's artlessly theatrical manner in company that endeared him to the writer. Though never published, Dickens left a comic little portrait of George written in the character of Sarah Gamp. She arrives at a railway office laden with her belongings, 'drove about like a brute animal and almost worrited into fits' when:

> . . . a gentleman with a large shirt-collar, and a hook nose, and a eye like one of Mr Sweedlepipe's hawks, and long locks of hair, and whiskers that I

wouldn't have no lady as I was engaged to meet suddenly a-turning round a corner, for any sum of money you could offer me, says laughing 'Halloa Mrs Gamp, what are you up to?' I didn't know him from a man (except by his clothes): but I says faintly, 'If you're a Christian man, show me where to get a second-cladge ticket for Manjester and have me put in a carriage, or I shall drop.' Which he kindly did, in a cheerful kind of way, skipping about in the strangest manner as ever I see, making all kinds of actions, and vinking at me from under the brim of his hat. . . .

She is informed by her companion in the carriage that this had been none other than 'The great George, ma'am. The Crookshanks.' Then she turns her head 'and sees the wery man a-making picturs of me on his thumb nail, at the winder!'

Dickens's next work after *Sketches by Boz* was *The Pickwick Papers*, which, since the original commission was only to provide a text to accompany a series of sporting prints by Robert Seymour, did not involve George (who was anyway still occupied with Boz). As it turned out it was Dickens's much broader conception of the annals of the Pickwick Club that prevailed, and when the artist committed suicide after only two parts had been published the number of illustrations was halved and handed over to an almost unknown illustrator, Hablot Browne. With the remarkable success of Pickwick, Boz (as he was still known) became a valuable literary property, and although his publishers, Chapman and Hall, rapidly commissioned a sequel, it was Richard Bentley who made the smarter move – by offering Dickens the editorship of a projected magazine, *Bentley's Miscellany*, in which his short stories and monthly serials could be published.

The *Miscellany* opened its pages in January 1837. They contained the first of Dickens's *Mudfog Sketches* illustrated by George and in this instance author and artist had unquestionably mulled the idea over in advance, since a hasty note from Dickens in November informed George he had been unable to write anything yet, and invited him to suggest an illustration. Likewise, in early January Dickens is writing again to arrange a conference on the illustrations for the opening episode of the new serial, *Oliver Twist* (which began in the February issue). And almost to the end of the serial, two years later, their collaboration proceeded equably, with the author scrupulously keeping the artist informed of the progress of 'their charge'. For instance, Dickens wrote to Cruikshank in November 1837: 'Shall you be at home at two o'clock today? I have been prevented from writing Oliver, so perhaps had better settle the Illustration with you at that time if convenient.'* In fact the greatest threat to *Oliver* was occasioned by a contractual dispute between Dickens and Bentley in the summer of 1837 – which came to a head with the author (temporarily) resigning his editorship. In the heat of the crisis George attempted to mediate between both injured parties, firing off letters to Bentley in his best semi-formal style, but finding his friend standing well and truly on principle. 'I would give *you* a call with pleasure,' Dickens wrote to George, 'but if it be on Mr Bentley's behalf, I would rather receive a more formal communication.'

It was only at the end of the last volume that disagreements over the illustrations began to sprout. The final batch of drawings were ready for the press when Dickens, who had been out of London, saw them for the first time. He immediately took violent objection to several of them, and two in particular: 'Sykes attempting to destroy his dog' and 'Rose Maylie and Oliver'. Of the latter plate his friend John Forster wrote to Bentley describing it unkindly as 'a Rowland Macasser frontispiece to a sixpenny book of forfeits'.* Dickens was rather gentler when he wrote to George, merely asking if he objected to re-designing this plate (he made no effort to get the Sykes plate changed). George's reaction is not recorded, except that he attempted first of all to 'improve' the old plate with additional detail and lots of stippling,* then gave up and etched a new design, 'Rose and Oliver at Agnes's tomb', which is what appeared in the *Miscellany* and all editions thereafter. (It was too late to prevent the original, so-called 'fireside plate' being published in the first edition of volume three which, strangely, had appeared before the end of the serial).

It is anticipating events to consider, at this point, George's claims concerning the 'origination' of *Oliver Twist* – for these did not come to light in England until 1870, when the artist was almost eighty and Dickens himself dead. Yet it is a literary issue which has exercised scholars, at least Dickens scholars, for a century and has hung like a miasma over George's reputation ever since. It is time to get the matter into perspective.

First, it is necessary to dispose of the claims Cruikshank did *not* make, which in the chorus of critical indignation have somehow accreted to the real issues. George did *not* claim to have 'written' *Oliver Twist* nor ever to have suggested *Pickwick* as, for instance, *The Dickens Encyclopedia* (1973) suggests. What George did claim openly – in a letter to *The Times* – was that he proposed the bare outline of a plot to Dickens and in some specific instances made concrete suggestions about characterisation and location. This was the extent of his public claims: privately, in a letter to an acquaintance, he also made the characteristically sweeping assertion that *Oliver Twist* was 'entirely my own idea and suggestion, and all the characters are mine'.* It is not intended to dismiss this difficult letter as a delusion of George's dotage, but it does require two immediate qualifications. First, it was written some time before the controversy became public in Britain and therefore before George was required to sort out in his mind the details of their collaboration as he saw it. But perhaps more to the point, George was temperamentally prone to overstatement in everything he did – it was what made him a great caricaturist and a bad actor – and exaggeration is a very different matter to wilful mendacity.

Let it also be said that George did not spontaneously publish his claims: they were made in his own defence, in the wake of a squabble between two of Dickens's biographers. The sequence of events ran as follows. In 1865, a Dr Shelton Mackenzie had written of Cruikshank as the originator of *Oliver Twist* in an American magazine, a statement based on a conversation he had had with the artist some twenty years before. In 1870 he was quoted in a life of Dickens (Hotten's), and that same year repeated his assertion in his own biography of Dickens. In 1871, however, there appeared a passionate denial in the first volume of yet another biography, by John Forster – the same who had been so scathing of George's illustrations. It was *this* rebuttal that moved George to write to *The Times* on 30 December 1871. Forster returned to the fray in his second volume of biography (1872), and George later that year in his pamphlet 'The Artist and the Author', but without adding much to what he had said in *The Times*.

According to George's letter, the idea he suggested to Dickens was 'the life of a London boy' who would be raised in the story 'from a most humble position up to a high and respectable one – in fact to illustrate one of those cases of common occurrence where men of humble origin, by natural ability, industry honest and honourable conduct, raise themselves to first-class positions in society'. Oliver, of course, was not a London boy, nor is this the story Dickens wrote: in fact as a synopsis (as John Harvey has pointed out*) it is closer to Hogarth's 'Industrious Apprentice' than *Oliver Twist*.

If that was the extent of his claim, even his critics would allow George to have suggested *a* plot to the author. But now he grows more specific: wishing 'to bring the habits and manners of the thieves of London before the public' he proposed the boy should fall among thieves, and to this end 'described the full-grown thieves [the Bill Sykeses] and their female companions, also the young thieves [the Artful Dodgers] and the receivers of stolen goods. . . . I had, a long time previously to this, directed Mr Dickens's attention to Field Lane, Holborn Hill, wherein resided many thieves and receivers of stolen goods, and it was suggested that one of these receivers, a Jew, should be introduced into the story.' George then relates how, on one occasion, when Dickens and Harrison Ainsworth were present, he described and performed the character of one such Jewish receiver – in fact Fagin. It is worth noting that Jerrold was of the opinion that George had found the model for Fagin in Petticoat Lane. Others remarked how similar Fagin – especially in the famous 'condemned cell' plate – was to George himself, and around this idea there grew up an often-repeated story of how the artist had conceived the drawing in the first place. He had despaired (so Horace Mayhew said) of ever capturing the Jew's wild, haunted look in the death-cell, and sat biting his knuckles in agitation on the edge of his bed. Suddenly he happened to catch sight of himself in the mirror, and realised he was unconsciously modelling the terrified prisoner himself, the crouching posture, staring eyes and all. George never exactly denied using himself as a model but told Frederick Locker – the patron of his later years – that it had been far less of an accident than the legend suggested.

Now if George were making that up, it was extremely rash of him gratuitously to introduce Ainsworth as a witness, since that gentleman was still living and in a position to deny the account (which he did not). At all events George's familiarity with the flotsam of London's underworld was undisputed, and testified to by many a published sketch of its less wholesome characters. There is, for example, in the third plate of *Scraps and Sketches*, published in 1828, a portrait of 'A Gentleman intended for the Bar' (i.e. the dock), a ruffian whose features are almost identical to those of Bill Sykes. The crumpled nose is the same, the twisted mouth, the sprouting hair on the chin, the wild staring eyes, the necktie knotted below an open shirt, and above all – the hallmark of Sykes – the straggling horns of hair on either side of the face. Here is the prototype of Sykes nine years before his creation.

Out of George's extensive gallery of rogues one other is, perhaps, of more than passing interest – the juvenile pickpocket, the artful dodger of London's streets. He was a favourite subject for George's pencil, cropping up as early as 1818 in the mêlée outside Hatchets in 'The Piccadilly Nuisance' (as a Jewish boy), and again the next year as a light-fingered link-boy in 'Foggy Weather'. His most recent manifestations, before *Oliver Twist*, were in George's illustrations to the *Comic Almanack*, where he appears with almost obsessive regularity: at St Bartholomew's Fair in the drawing for September 1835 (a pair of lads working the side-shows), in 'Transfer Day at the Bank' February 1836 (a rather older version), among the milling crowds on Ludgate Hill on 'Lord Mayor's Day' (1836) – close scrutiny will reveal several of them on the job in this plate.

Simple observation suggests this breed of apprentice thief had long been on the artist's mind, and a letter from George to Mackenzie confirms that this was so. In it he writes:

> . . . but whilst writing this letter I may just mention that I have now before
> me the list which I showed you of the proposed illustrations for *The Life of a*
> *London Thief* – with some of the sketches – all of which were done when
> Charles Dickens was a little boy – some 15 years before I ever saw or heard
> of him.*

These were the sketches that Mackenzie said, in the American journal, he had seen on a visit to Myddleton Terrace and which Cruikshank said Dickens had also seen before *Oliver Twist* was written. Until recently the existence of any such 'list' was unknown, but deep in the voluminous files of the Victoria & Albert Museum Professor Vogler has unearthed it, a sheet of sketches and lists of notes.* They are clearly what George later wrote on the page: 'intended to illustrate *The Life of a Thief*', with lists of underworld slang, references to other works on criminals, and a sketched outline of an 'early life' among other visual notations. Several visual references to other work George was doing at the time point to a date somewhere around 1819, or indeed 'some 15 years before I ever saw or heard' of Charles Dickens.

To return for a moment to the artist's claims in *The Times*: he points out that the illustrated appearance of *Oliver Twist* changes radically after the second issue, maintaining that this was in consequence of a current scandal in the parish of St James's, Westminster, where several farmed-out orphans had died in the appalling conditions of the local workhouse. It was George's slightly sentimental idea to change Oliver's appearance from the 'queer kind of chap' Dickens wanted, to a 'nice pretty boy', to enlist public sympathy for other workhouse-boys. This overnight transformation *did* take place between the February and March issues – perhaps at the instigation of George's close friend Joseph Pettigrew, the man who had first made the workhouse scandal public. Dickens obviously acceded to this, but it was not a modification that affected the story in any way.

George's final observation in *The Times* was that 'long before *Oliver Twist* was ever thought of . . . I had made a sketch of one of the condemned cells in Newgate Prison; as I had a great object in letting the public see what sort of place these cells were and how they were furnished, and also to show a wretched condemned criminal therein, I thought it desirable to introduce such a subject into this work'. He adds that he had the greatest difficulty in persuading Dickens, but at length the wretched Fagin was selected for the role. In the British Museum there is such a sketch: it does not portray Fagin, nor Sykes (as the handwritten caption states) but it *is* of a prisoner in the condemned cell and lends weight to the notion that the artist was keen to see a final episode in the death-cell. George's account, incidentally, also offers a simple explanation for the unconvincing way in which Fagin is brought to the extreme penalty in the book: that the decision that the Jew should swing for his misdeeds was taken too late in the story's development for even remotely plausible evidence against him to be written in.

In most scholarly dissertations on the Cruikshank–Dickens controversy it is uncritically assumed that the artist had no right to be plying the author with suggestions. But that is not how George, steeped as we have seen in an older tradition of collaboration, interpreted his role. That there were discussions in the course of *Oliver Twist*'s creation, we have Dickens's own evidence; and that George came to these discussions as an authority on the subject and with some already well-formulated ideas is demonstrated by much of his published and unpublished work.

What we do not know is the extent to which Dickens might have been influenced by these ideas. He was still alive when Mackenzie published the claims in America – and was actually in the States two years later – but made no public comment on them (could he *really* not have known about them?). The burden of refutation rests with John Forster, and his abrupt denial is supported only by the fact that Dickens wrote the last few chapters of the book 'in a lump' before George got round to illustrating them, and subsequently asked him to re-design the 'fireside plate'. What relevance this has to George's claims, which mostly concern the initial stages of the book, one might well ask. And Forster – as his cavalier sub-editing of Dickens's letters for his biography, and his wholesale destruction of precious correspondence, show – is no great ally in any quest for truth. It no more befitted Forster to accuse George of inventing 'a wonderful story' than anyone else since, in the deafening absence of proof.

In spite of Forster's pyromania, enough of the correspondence between George Cruikshank and Charles Dickens has survived to reveal the warmth of their early friendship. There are regular visits to the opera and theatre together, and once to an 'exhibition of mesmerism', trips down to Broadstairs where the Dickens family spent their summers, sittings for a portrait by George, and no end of dinner-parties at Doughty Street, and later Devonshire Terrace. As a connoisseur of characters, his friend's eccentricities positively appealed to Dickens. In an affectionate aside he wrote of him:*

> George has enormous whiskers which straggle all down his throat in such weather, and stick out in front of him, like a partially unravelled bird's-nest; so that he looks queer enough at the best, but when he is very wet and

in a state between jollity (he is always very jolly with me) and the deepest gravity (going to a funeral, you know) it is utterly impossible to resist him: especially as he makes the strangest remarks the mind of man can conceive, without any intention of being funny, but rather meaning to be philosophical.*

Dickens himself could respond to, even become infected by, George's almost boyish ebullience – 'my dear Georgius' he would start his letters and sign off 'heartily yours', a breach in formality he permitted himself only with close friends – but not everyone was as happy to indulge George's quirks, as Dickens was aware when he wrote to Ainsworth: 'Cruikshank has been here to say that he thought your dinner was last Saturday, how that he finds it is *next* Saturday, and how he means to come with me and surprise you. As the surprise, however agreeable, might be too much for Mrs Touchet, I have thought it best to send you this warning. Mind, you must assume the virtue though you have it not, and feign extravagant astonishment at the sight of the Illustrious George!'*

Oliver Twist was the only one of Dickens's novels that George illustrated. While it was in progress they had worked together, for Bentley, on a *Life of Grimaldi*, George's old Islington friend who had died earlier in 1837. Dickens's role was simply that of editing someone else's manuscript – which he found hard going and complained of as 'dreary twaddle' (unlike the artist he was not old enough to recall vividly Joe's inimitable style and famous leap). In the normal course of events George would have illustrated Dickens's next serial for Bentley – which was to have been *Barnaby Rudge* – but even as the final instalments of Oliver were appearing in the *Miscellany* Dickens was once more entering the lists against his publisher. He believed Bently had exploited him over *Oliver Twist*, and refused point blank to begin the new novel until offered better terms: obtaining little or no satisfaction, he thankfully resigned the editorship of the *Miscellany* at the end of January 1839. *Barnaby Rudge* was completed but not until 1841, by which time it was earmarked for serialisation in Dickens's own magazine *Master Humphrey's Clock*, whose regular illustrators were Phiz and George Cattermole. Conscious no doubt that he had left George in the lurch, the author proposed that the two of them launch an Annual together, but by then George was too deeply involved in a project of his own and therefore declined, adding what turned out to be an ironic postscript: 'It is of no use expressing my regret that we are not working together (as we ought to have done from the first) – and should this said speculation of mine unfortunately fail – I shall be ready to join you in any way, and work on if agreeable, to the last.'* There were two further collaborations between them: a slim volume of 'The Loving Ballad of Lord Bateman' (1839), a comic enshrinement of

George's by now celebrated party piece, with a commentary by Dickens which he insisted remain anonymous; then in 1841 George donated some illustrations to *The Pic-Nic Papers*, an anthology edited by Dickens for the relief of the widow of John Macrone (the publisher of Boz, who died in September 1837).

The new editor of *Bentley's Miscellany* was William Harrison Ainsworth, another rising literary 'lion' – both professionally as a creator of dashing historical romances, and socially as the centre of an equally dashing artistic circle that gathered at his home, Kensal Lodge. To date his reputation was based largely on his saga of Dick Turpin, *Rookwood*, which had gone into many editions. George had been brought in to illustrate the fourth edition in 1836, an inauspicious start, as it happened, to their erratic partnership. Ainsworth somewhat dogmatically pronounced George's designs to be 'sketchy' and protested to Macrone, the publisher: 'They are anything but full subjects and appear to be chosen as much as possible for light work. He shirked the inauguration scene, for instance, because it was too crowded. I quite agree with you that a few good designs are better than many meagre sketches, and all I want is that you should make George understand this. . . . I pray of you to see George Cruikshank and don't let him put us off so badly – there's a good fellow!'*

Macrone evidently didn't share this patronising view, for he straightaway advertised George as the illustrator of Ainsworth's forthcoming œuvre, *The Lions of London*. Ainsworth pleaded for John Leech to be engaged as well – 'let Leech undertake the old – the romantic – the picturesque; George, the modern comedy and manners',* but in the event it was an academic point, since the author failed to produce a book for either of them to illustrate. Ainsworth's contract with Bentley, however, required him to produce a serial, on the same terms as Dickens had done, and this did materialise, as *Jack Sheppard* (a tale of yet another archetypal English brigand), which ran in the *Miscellany* through 1839.

Its success was phenomenal. Whatever shortcomings Ainsworth may have had as a stylist, he could tell a cracking good yarn. It was pirated for the stage by half-a-dozen theatres, *Jack Sheppard* ballads and song-sheets proliferated, its catch-phrases could be heard on every street corner. As usual author and artist had to content themselves with the fame, for no fortune came their way (except that George was commissioned to 'superintend' the scene-painting at the Surrey Theatre). Thackeray, somewhat biased against Ainsworth, remarked 'it seems to us that Mr Cruikshank really created the tale and that Mr Ainsworth as it were only put words to it . . . let any man look at that second plate of the murder on the Thames, and he must acknowledge how much more brilliant the artist's description is than the writer's'.* There was no need to belabour the author for his part in this, but it is true that George's drawings are among his best, showing once more how he could rise to a subject close to his heart and which allowed him such a broad historical canvas. George Augustus Sala recalled how, many years later, George took him on a guided tour of the scenes of the (real) Jack Sheppard's exploits – the ale-house in Drury Lane when Jack first met Edgeworth Bess, the site of his first burglary in White Horse Yard, the tavern in Clare Market where he had his final revel. 'George was a walking Directory in low-life London,' proclaimed Sala, 'and was one of the few men who could tell you anything definite about Great Swallow Street, the site of the present Regent Street,'* but as for the carpenter's shop in Wych Street where the rascal had supposedly carved his name on the beam, the artist had considerable doubts about the authenticity of that particular episode.

Ainsworth's preoccupation with villains, and the fact that his novels (like *Oliver Twist*) had been illustrated by Cruikshank, led to some rather sniffy diatribes in the high-brow periodicals against the new 'gallows' school of writers and the 'Newgate novel', but the fact was that *Jack Sheppard* had added substantially to the circulation of the *Miscellany*. It was followed, hot-foot, by another historical pageant of derring-do, *Guy Fawkes* (1840) – as had been stipulated in Ainsworth's original contract. Meanwhile, the author and artist were hatching arrangements for a serial of their own, *The Tower of London*, which for more profitable terms they would allow Mr Bentley to publish outside the *Miscellany*. The new contract made Cruikshank and Ainsworth sole and equal partners in the work, with the publisher simply receiving a third share of the profits.

This agreement between George and Ainsworth was to have wider implications later on, but its immediate effect was to make the artist highly dissatisfied with the rates he was getting from Bentley for his illustrations in the *Miscellany*. It is obvious he had started complaining to the proprietor in January 1840, for Dickens notes that they were quarrelling even then, but the feud came to a head in March when Bentley took exception to the work George was doing for *Guy Fawkes*, and another serial running concurrently called *Stanley Thorn*. In great dudgeon George confided in Ainsworth:

> I had just got home when I was honor'd by a visit from Mr Bentley, who expressed considerable displeasure at the plates for the *Guy* and *Stanley Thorn* and gave me to understand that he should employ another artist in Miscellany besides myself. Upon this I declined having anything further to do with it, upon which he took his leave not, however, without a great deal of *hot breath* being expended on both sides. . . . I shall be very glad if I can be really quit of him.*

To what extent this was a negotiating ploy by Bentley is impossible to say. Rumour had it that George was deliberately producing poor work in order to force the publisher to release him, but a glance at the plates does not really bear that out. They are not especially good, but nor are they particularly bad: the illustrations for *Stanley Thorn* betray a certain sparseness of detail, which Bentley may have compared unfavourably with the rich and precise scenes from *The Tower of London* and considered he was getting short measure. At all events Ainsworth intervened with a warning that 'I will not allow Mr Leech or any other artist than Mr Cruikshank to illustrate any portion of the work',* and there matters stood until the end of the year with George – still in a temper – producing his monthly quota.

But the following year brought another blow to George's pride. As a follow-up to their successful private enterprise with *The Tower of London* Cruikshank had suggested the Fire of London as a fertile source for a new story, and Ainsworth had apparently concurred. Even Ellis, Ainsworth's biographer, grants that George suggested such an idea 'in the absence of contradiction from A'. It was a shock therefore to discover that the author, tempted by a lucrative offer from *The Sunday Times*, then proceeded to make the Fire his setting for a serial (*Old St Paul's*) in that paper, where of course no illustrations could be published.

1841 was a bad year altogether. His distemper with Bentley continued to make work on the *Miscellany* a drudge, his fruitful partnership with Ainsworth was dissolved, at the end of the year his wife Mary became dangerously ill, and his own publishing brain-child (the *Omnibus*, of which more later) which had been born in May with such great promise was clearly dying in its infancy. It was at this point that George's oldest friend came to his aid: Joseph Pettigrew had known him since the days at Dorset Street and in due course had become the family doctor. Since then, he had achieved eminence as a bibliophile, a surgeon to royalty, a reformer, and a leading Egyptologist (George had illustrated his *History of Egyptian Mummies* in 1834). Although only a year older he was, according to Jerrold, 'among the few who exercised a little authority over the turbulent and self-willed George'. Clearly this kindly gentleman realised (perhaps while attending Mary) the despondency into which the artist had sunk, and determined to do what he could. Voluntarily he assumed the role of mediator between George and Ainsworth, whom he knew had left the *Miscellany* and was in the process of setting up his own magazine. Reading between the lines of George's account, he was obviously a man of consummate tact: 'To my utter astonishment, my friend Pettigrew called upon me one day with a message from Mr W. Harrison Ainsworth, to this effect, that he (Mr Ainsworth) was extremely sorry that there had been any unpleasantness between us, and that if I would forgive him, and be friends, nothing of this kind should ever happen again.'

The gist of the reconciliation was an offer that George should join forces with him once again in his new endeavour, *Ainsworth's Magazine*. 'To this most unexpected proposition at first I would not listen,' the headstrong artist went on. 'But as my friend Pettigrew kept on for some time urging me to be friends with Mr Ainsworth . . . I *did* forgive Mr Ainsworth and agree to work with him again.' Honour satisfied and pride salved, George devoted himself single-mindedly to the new project, even to the extent of publicising his final rupture with Bentley in a later issue of *Ainsworth's Magazine*:

> Mr George Cruikshank is happy to inform his Friends and his Public that he has ceased to have any connexion whatever with *Bentley's Miscellany* – He therefore begs them to observe that, from this date, there will not appear *under any circumstances* any illustration, either on wood, copper or steel executed by him for that Publication; and that AINSWORTH'S MAGAZINE will be, henceforth, the *only* magazine illustrated by him.

This appeared in the November 1842 issue, but notwithstanding, George continued to provide plates for Bentley until the end of the year, including some delightful etchings for Barham's *Ingoldsby Legends*, which had been appearing from time to time in the *Miscellany*.

Over the next three years Ainsworth and Cruikshank excavated still deeper into the mines of history with *The Miser's Daughter* (1842) a tale of avarice set in the dark days of the Jacobite uprising, *Windsor Castle* (1843) the tragic story of Anne Boleyn, and *St James's* (1844) featuring Queen Anne and the redoubtable Duke of Marlborough. By now George had begun regularly engraving on steel plates, a medium offering scope for both delicacy and drama, and in these books he demonstrated his total control over it, with astonishing gradations of light and shade and a facility in his crowded set-pieces that was never equalled. Increasingly as the series progressed George abandoned all traces of caricature in favour of complete naturalism, so that the illustrations for *Windsor Castle* in particular have the epic quality of grand historical painting. Yet while we can admire the sheer technical range here of George's etching, it must be admitted that this elevated style has drained the warmth and humanity out of his work.

George would probably not have agreed, seeing here some vindication of Lockhart's ill-advised claim that he could 'design as many Annunciations, Beatifications, Apotheoses, Metamorphoses and so forth, as would cover York Cathedral from end to end'. Over the next few years there were to be other opportunities for Cruikshank to explore this genre further, notably in his melodramatic designs for Maxwell's *History of the Irish Rebellion* (1845), but after the publication of *St James's*, the partnership with Ainsworth, to George's disappointment, once more disintegrated, with the sale of the magazine. George afterwards intimated that this had been in breach of some tacit understanding between them, and once more grew thoroughly disillusioned. Yet again Pettigrew attempted to reconcile the two men, but this time found the artist adamant – he would not work with Ainsworth again. 'My friend the doctor', said George, recalling the interview, 'found it was not at all necessary to *feel* my pulse; for he could plainly *see* it beat rather fiercely.'

Many of those who have dismissed George's testimony on *Oliver Twist* as pure fantasy point to his retrospective claims to have originated two of Ainsworth's novels as well, as reinforcement of their view that the artist in old age was suffering from senile delusions of grandeur. In truth it would have suited their argument better if they had *not* done so. For the weight of evidence – notwithstanding Ainsworth's airy disclaimers – is overwhelmingly on George's side.

Once again we have to step forward twenty-eight years to reach the root cause of the controversy: in April 1872 a dramatisation of *The Miser's Daughter* was staged at the Adelphi theatre, the scenes based on the etchings in the book, but advertised without any reference to George's connection with the work. As a visual realisation of the story, he felt the drama owed some acknowledgement to him (the original visualiser of the story) – and said so in a mild letter to *The Times*.* He underlined his case by adding that it was he who had suggested 'the first idea' to Ainsworth, as well as its Jacobite setting ('as all my ancestors were mixed up in the rebellion of '45'). Ainsworth's response, a few days later, was merely to deny it and suppose Cruikshank 'to be labouring under a singular delusion'. George's blood was up now: in a second letter he repeated his claim and enlarged it by revealing that he had been the 'sole originator' of *The Tower of London* as well, hinting darkly at a work he was preparing for the press which would give 'a full, true and particular account of all the professional transactions between Mr Ainsworth and myself'. Ainsworth's final rejoinder, before the Editor closed the correspondence, was to brand George's assertions as 'preposterous'.

Ainsworth did subsequently make one long statement about the controversy, in a letter to Jerrold, Cruikshank's biographer, for publication in his book. Unaccountably, Jerrold allowed it to stand without comment, but for all its length it contained almost nothing to contradict George. Here are the only remotely relevant passages:

> I desire to state emphatically, that not a single line – not a word – in any of my novels was written by their illustrator, Cruikshank. In no instance did he even see a proof. The subjects were arranged with him early in the

month, and about the fifteenth he used to send me tracings of the plates. That was all. . . . Had Cruikshank been capable of constructing a story why did he not exercise his talent when he had no connection with Mr Dickens or myself? . . . But overweening vanity formed a strong part of Cruikshank's character. He boasted so much of the assistance he had rendered authors, that at last he believed he had written their works. Moreover he was excessively troublesome and obtrusive with his suggestions. . . . It would be unjust, however, to deny that there was wonderful cleverness and quickness about Cruikshank, and I am indebted to him for many valuable hints and suggestions.

Ainsworth entirely misses the point. George never claimed to have 'written' anyone's work, nor to have any special talent for writing. He would certainly have agreed with Ainsworth's outline of their monthly working schedule, and as for the 'obtrusiveness' of his suggestions, he might quite fairly have observed that at the time Ainsworth seemed remarkably grateful for them.

George's promised account, *The Artist and the Author*, was published as a pamphlet towards the end of 1872. In it he covered all the novels of Ainsworth he had illustrated (seven in all), but in only two of these did he make any claims to origination: *The Miser's Daughter* and *The Tower of London*, going into particular details on his part in the development of the latter. He began by pointing out that in *The Tower of London* he and Ainsworth had been equal partners – an unusual arrangement in any circumstances, and most unlikely if the artist was supposed to be playing a subordinate role. He then maintained that it was he who had first suggested a story based on the last days of Lady Jane Grey *not*, as Ainsworth's biographer supposed in his 'refutation', a story based on the Tower itself, which was only the setting not the subject of the novel. He went on:

> I then told him that I had long since seen the room in the Tower where that beautiful and accomplished lady was imprisoned, and other parts of the fortress . . . and if he would then go with me to the Tower, I would show these places to him. He at once accepted my offer, and off we went to Hungerford Stairs, now the site of the Charing Cross Railway Station, and whilst waiting on the beach for a boat to go to London Bridge we met there my dear friend, the late W. Jerdan, who enquired where we were going to. My reply was that I was taking Mr Ainsworth a prisoner to the Tower. . . .

In fact, George and Ainsworth thereafter made monthly visits to the Tower, with the artist making voluminous sketches (which are in the British Museum) of every nook and cranny of the fortifications, and supplying them to the author for reference. Being a serial the novel was, in effect, written scene by scene and the procedure according to George was as follows:

I have now most distinctly to state that Mr Ainsworth wrote up to most of my suggestions and designs, although some of the subjects we jointly arranged, to introduce into the work; and I used every month to send him the tracings or outlines of the sketches or drawings from which I was making the etchings to illustrate the work, *in order that he might write up to them*, and that they should be accurately described. And I beg the reader to understand that all these etchings or plates were ready for publication before the letterpress was printed, and sometimes even before the author had written in manuscript. . . .

This is the most crucial part of George's evidence. He is saying, in brief, that the illustrations preceded the text in most cases. Now the readers of his pamphlet (if there were any) had only his word to rely on: we fortunately have the confirmation of such of the correspondence as has survived.

These letters, quoted in full in the Appendix, show George was telling no less than the truth. They describe incidents in the novel which George had worked out down to the last detail, and which Ainsworth in virtually every case we know about followed closely, adding surprisingly little (as John Harvey, who was entirely responsible for seeing the significance of the letters, points out). Nor are they simply the 'valuable hints' Ainsworth would have had us believe: they are central and climactic episodes worked out at length and with care. It is not entirely surprising that the author should have come to rely so much on George's directions: the poor man, after all, was writing another novel – *Guy Fawkes* – at the same time, a burden that Dickens himself found hard enough. What is 'preposterous' is that he should have glossed over his collaborator's claims so blissfully. It is also worth pointing out, perhaps, that their correspondence shows George to have made a far larger contribution to *Jack Sheppard* than he made out.

The judgements that were made on George's claims by many of his contemporaries are those which have been transmitted, uncritically, almost to the present time. But the fact is that Cruikshank's reputation in his own day was against him: his associates knew him for a lovable eccentric, a reformed drunk (as they supposed), a man of impulse. It did not seem to them likely, or respectable, that his assertions, however precise and emphatic, could stand up against even the woolly depositions of Ainsworth – not to mention the arrogant irrelevancies of Forster. George had lived too long: few knew about, or cared about, the tradition in which he had been brought up, and those men who might have come to his support were long since dead. So, as far as his literary contributions were concerned, he was written off as senile and deluded, and has remained so. He is owed better than that.

6 Morals for the Millions
(1835-1848)

The distinctions between journalism and literature that seem so obvious to us today were, in early Victorian London, by no means so clear-cut. Not only were novels regularly published in periodical form, but their authors were almost invariably the founder, proprietor or editor of a magazine at some stage in their careers. Dickens on the *Miscellany* and Ainsworth on *Ainsworth's Magazine*, as we have seen, combined their two roles most profitably, but they were no more than echoing the pattern of many of their contemporaries. Frederick Marryat had his *Metropolitan Magazine* and Thomas Hood his *Comic Annual*; Gilbert à Beckett became famous through his *Figaro in London*, while Douglas Jerrold edited the *Illuminated Magazine* and Thackeray the *National Standard*. Artists, too, relied heavily on monthly journalism: William Heath monopolised the pages of the *Looking-Glass*, and *McLean's Monthly* was simply a vehicle for Robert Seymour's sketches, and later John Doyle's.

For Cruikshank, the opportunity arrived in 1834. That year the stamp duty on almanacks was repealed, opening the flood-gates on a deluge of almanacks of every conceivable degree of utility: bijou almanacks for the drawing-room, miniature ones for the waistcoat, even circular ones for the crown of the hat and almanacks printed on pocket handkerchiefs! Most of these proved as ephemeral as the fashion that had begotten them, but a few sturdier creations took root and prospered and among these was the *Comic Almanack*, published by Charles Tilt and edited by the elder Vizetelly. It ran from 1835 to 1853 and in its bizarre pages may be found contributions from Albert Smith, Thackeray, à Beckett, Henry Mayhew and others: comic diaries, mock horoscopes, poems, satires on learned societies, astringent comments on passing conceits and fancies. But its chief ornament was George's series of etchings, some two hundred and fifty of them over the period. It became in time his undisputed domain, a reflection of his quizzical view of the world and a harmless refuge for his wilder fancies.

In the *Comic Almanack* all the most amiable aspects of George's genius flow together: the mockery is good-natured, the prejudices well-mannered, the satire inoffensive in deference to mid-nineteenth century sensibilities – a symptom also, it could be said, of George's own mellowing convictions (all the editor's keen suggestions for political plates fell on stony ground). What the *Almanack* offered the artist was a framework free from the literary restraints of his books, but more enduring than his prints; and his legacy is a compelling portrait of two decades in London.

The London of the early issues is still a city of hansom cabs and omnibus cads, of clerks with quill pens behind their ears, of pleasure-gardens frequented in a desperate search for new diversions, beadles beating the boundaries of their parishes, and the drawing-room perils of the Polka. The later years have brought the railways into the very heart of the metropolis, department stores with windows storeys high, the crinoline with its complex infrastructure of wire and whalebone. Great events and week-long wonders are all tossed together in George's *Almanack* like a huge mixed salad – the triumphal procession of young Victoria's coronation, the idiotic craze for water cures, the penny post, the passion-killing progress of Mrs Bloomer's dress reform.

When the national competition for the design of the frescoes to decorate Barry's new Houses of Parliament was in full swing in 1843, George pops up in person in the *Almanack* offering the authorities his own uplifting design. The reason it was rejected (he claims) was that it was too big to get through the archway. But could it have had anything to do with the fact that it was a gargantuan memorial to Guy Fawkes? Only occasionally do flashes of the old indignation intrude: in the spring of 1846 the sensation of London had been the visit of the famous American midget Tom Thumb, who had put himself on display at the Egyptian Hall and lived regally on the proceeds from the multitudes that came to gawk at him. At the same time in a different part of the building the artist Benjamin Haydon had been holding an exhibition of his work, past which the crowds had swept heedless and uncaring. A few weeks later Haydon had killed himself in front of an unstarted canvas – a circumstance that moved George to a bitter comment on public tastes, 'Born a Genius, Born a Dwarf'.

For nearly twenty years the *Almanack* provided George with a regular, if hardly princely, income. It died in the end of its own ossification, purveying, at least in its text, the same 'merry quips and oddities' with which it had started; but its early promise tempted its publisher Charles Tilt (or more probably his new young partner, David Bogue) to add a monthly magazine to his stable, also with George as its figurehead. *George Cruikshank's Omnibus*, which began its journey in May 1841, was the direct result of the artist's dispute with Bentley (in the matter of remuneration for his work on the *Miscellany*) which had been rumbling on since the previous January, and of his breach with Ainsworth who had defected to *The Sunday Times*. As he explained to Ainsworth in March,* he had waited for three months to begin work on their next joint project, the novel based on the Fire of London.

. . . what conclusion was I to come to but that you had *cut* me. At the latter end of last year, you announced that *we* were preparing a New Work! In the early part of December last I saw an advertisement that *your* New Work was to be published in The Sunday Times. You do not come to me, or send for me, nor send me any explanation. I meet you at Dickens's on New Year's Eve. You tell me then that you will see me in a few days and explain everything to my satisfaction. I hear nothing from you. I purposely keep myself disengaged, refusing many advantageous offers of work – still I hear nothing from you . . . I then conclude that you do not intend to join me in any New Work and therefore determine to do something for myself – indeed I could hold out no longer.

If injured pride, as George seems to be suggesting, was the driving force behind the *Omnibus*, that might account for the slightly apologetic approach he adopted to the whole project. In February he had written to Dickens of the possibility of his 'speculation' failing, and when Ainsworth finally came up with a conciliatory request for George to illustrate *Old St Paul's* in book form, he turned it down – not because the *Omnibus* was going to take the publishing world by storm but because 'if I were to withdraw my projected publication I am sure that I would be a laughing-stock to some and – what is worse – I fear with others I should lose all title to honor or integrity'.*

The *Omnibus* lasted for just nine issues. It did not capture the public imagination and lost money from the start. There were some eye-catching moments, like George's macabre steel-engraving of *Jack O'Lantern* and the continuing travails of the susceptible Mrs Toddles (for ever in vain pursuit of the departing omnibus). But it was too personal to reach the kind of audience a monthly required – the first sixteen pages of the first issue were devoted to George; a preface, a portrait, a long essay correcting a recent profile of himself, and a comic article on his 'last pair of Hessian boots'. And perhaps there was also an uncomfortable overlap between the editorial ideas of George in the title role and his editor, Samuel Laman Blanchard, who seems to have been bombarded with a welter of well-intentioned directives.

But the most obvious cause of its decease was the arrival on the scene, in July 1841, of *Punch*, just two months after the *Omnibus*. The new magazine was bright and breezy from the first, slightly disrespectful but never distasteful (except to George), and found a wide market. The irony was that *Punch* had been the offspring of two of George's own colleagues, the journalist Henry Mayhew and the engraver Ebenezer Landells who had often worked on the artist's plates, and in its embryo days it owed many of its visual ideas to Cruikshank's well-worked formulae. Mark Lemon, the magazine's early editor, beseeched George to work for *Punch* – on his own terms if he liked – but met with absolutely no response. He objected, he said, to the 'inexcusable personalities' he had observed in the paper; which must have sounded a little hollow from the lips of a man who had been the scourge of politicians in his youth. Yet he meant it (and in fairness could have defied anyone to point to a personality from his own pencil in the last fifteen years that could not be justified by some didactic purpose). 'We shall have you yet,' Lemon persisted. 'Never!' retorted George, reportedly striking one of his theatrical attitudes.

Never, it turned out to be. When the *Omnibus* folded in January 1842 the last page carried the polite fiction that it was being merged with *Ainsworth's Magazine* as from next month, and would appear in its own right only as an Annual henceforth (a prediction that was never fulfilled). It is true that George never entirely lost faith in the old 'Buss' as Dickens had called it* (kindly praising the first issue as 'driv in a slap-up style, and altogether an uncommon spicy con-sarn', in the vernacular of the Cockney coachmen). When he and Ainsworth went their different ways in 1844, George had dreams of reviving the *Omnibus* and actually went down to the printers, Bradbury and Evans, to see what old stock they still held. Mentioning his plans to Bradbury he found a sympathetic ear, and although George was wisely dissuaded from putting the *Omnibus* back on the road, the printers did offer to go into partnership with him in a 'new illustrated periodical'. The advertisements, when they appeared at the end of 1844, had a distinctly tutorial air, with George and Gilbert à Beckett (the new editor) addressing their public from a platform. *George Cruikshank's Table-Book* it was called, and it stumbled on for a year before going under, and resurfacing after a fashion in April 1846 as *Our Own Times* for another four numbers. It might cheerfully have been consigned to oblivion but for two of the artist's large plates: the first, 'The Folly of Crime', shows just how far George's moralistic tendencies had developed. Some time later he actually stated his occupation as 'Drawing and Painting. To prevent evil and try to do good',* and would no doubt have cited this heavy allegory as one of his sterner attempts. This engraved sermon presents crime as a form of self-delusion, and the criminal as the time-honoured Fool complete with cap and bells: in its central panel the assassin is hurled into the abyss in pursuit of an illusory treasure, while the border is a series of sketched rubrics spelling out the mortifying consequences of lawlessness. That the picture was not without at least some power of suggestion can be assumed from the fact that shortly afterwards Thackeray (who was a contributor to the *Table-Book*) adopted this Fool motif for his illuminations to *Vanity Fair*.

The second plate, 'The Triumph of Cupid', would fill a psychiatrist's case-book. It is a fireside reverie, with George in smoking-jacket and dog on lap, puffing away at his long meerschaum – which he claimed acted 'as a conductor, along which flashes of inspiration are conveyed with every whiff'. Above him the swirling clouds of smoke are populated by the exhalations of his imagination, kings and chimney-sweeps, duchesses and clowns all in thrall to the little god of Love. For a pipe-dream the figures are wonderfully substantial, as if the artist's ideal, teeming, miniature world has taken over. Even George himself is *part* of it, an elfin alter ego painting (note, not etching) the contemplative figure in the chair. The diminutive artist, incidentally, is the only human in the picture not in chains – underlining the message that George tried to convey in many of his representations of himself, that is, the importance of the Artist. To digress a little it is worth noting that George's portraits of himself, which recur constantly in his published and unpublished work, laid him open to frequent charges of vanity from his contemporaries. George Somes Layard, who collated many of them, claimed that 'they were prompted by egotism ... it was one of the artist's methods of using the big, big I'*. George was certainly preoccupied with his appearance in public: Henry Vizetelly maintained it was vanity 'that led him in after-life to bring a long lock of his scanty hair forward to try and conceal his baldness, and secure it in its place with an elastic band, which he foolishly hoped would be invisible to the most searching glances'*. Scarcely any painted or etched portrait (even his self-portraits) satisfied him and he was always reluctant to have his photograph taken because, he said, the end-result always elongated his already long nose. (In fact, George had virtually a fixation about noses of any description: of all the parts of the anatomy that he thrusts before our attention in his drawings it is the nose that excels – there are men with two noses, or noses that won't stop growing, in 'Philoprogenitiveness' a whole weird-nosed family, in his *Sketchbook* a complete gallery of strange hooters. And the recurring idea of getting revenge by 'pulling a fellow's nose' surely harks back to a very early preoccupation with this particular organ.

But having said all this, what is often overlooked is that almost every time George introduces himself into a plate it is *as an artist*, as if he is trying to win the reader's recognition of the artist's status in, and contribution to, society. Some of the plates show how the 'artist' is ill-rewarded by society (*Hard Times*, 1814), exploited (*A Chapter of Noses*, 1834) or rejected (*Guy Fawkes*, 1844). Other plates, more positively, make a point of presenting him as an equal with the writer or publisher – as in his several frontispieces for Hone, Dickens, Ainsworth, à Beckett and other collaborators. On these terms it is closer to professional pride than to personal conceit.

Quite apart from the intrinsic interest of 'The Triumph of Cupid', it also represents one of the high-water marks of the engraver's art. Increasingly, published illustrations were being surrendered to the wood-engraver or the glyphographer, as the demands of increased circulation made steel-engraving more and more unprofitable.

Such exquisite elaboration as this and other plates in the *Table-Book* contain was to become one of the sacrifices of the art of illustration to the mass market.

While the *Table-Book* showed that given scope to develop a message George could apply the whole battery of his skills, the sustained trivialities of *The Comic Almanack* offered more security than personal satisfaction. It had not been going many years when Thackeray – usually so partisan for George – commented to a correspondent: 'Yesterday I had the misfortune to read *The Comic Almanack* – anything worse or more paltry cannot well be imagined – it is as bad, very nearly, as the prints which illustrate it: and these are odious. Cruikshank I suppose is tired of the thing. . . .'* That was rather a hasty judgement on these good-natured frivolities – to which he himself had contributed, in point of fact; and the added irony was that when George produced his first morality story in 1844, *The Bachelor's Own Book*, his inspiration may well have been Thackeray's contributions to the *Almanack*.

In the issues for 1839 and 1840, Thackeray had written a couple of light-hearted, short serial stories, *Stubbs's Calendar* and *Barber Cox*, and George's month-by-month engravings for these had been his major contribution for those years. His working procedure with Thackeray, incidentally, seems to have been very similar to that with Ainsworth: 'Here is a programme (of *Barber Cox*) which Wright and I concocted. . . . You may take any liberties, of course, and when you have done the first four plates I will make the writing,' the author wrote to him.* Both stories have basically the same theme, and one very pertinent to the social climate of the times: in each case the hero is a social climber seeking an entrée into society, with the money to do it but without the necessary graces or intelligence to know when he's being conned. Stubbs ends up as a street salesman and police informer, and Cox back in the barber's shop where he began. Stubbs sells the story of his adventures to a literary gentleman for a pint of beer, adding: 'He's a strange chap, and says they're *moral*. I'm blest if I can see anything moral in them.'

But George could, and the hero of his *Bachelor's Own Book*, one Mr Lambkin, suffers from all the pretensions and setbacks of Messrs Cox and Stubbs. The attractions of documenting the adventures of Lambkin 'in pursuit of pleasure and amusement and also a search of health and happiness' (as the sub-title put it) were twofold. First of all there was something of a vogue at the time in Paris for the narrative-illustrations of the caricaturist Rudolphe Topffer and his comic characters M. Jabot and M. Vieux-Bois (the latter was plagiarised in England as Mr Obadiah Oldbuck with great success). But, more important perhaps, here was a format that could accommodate a contemporary version of the Hogarthian 'progress' – which, quite apart from the moral content, had long been George's ideal of the Artist as Author.

'Let him proceed – and as he proceeds, let him think of Hogarth,' Lockhart had written of him twenty years earlier. There had been Hogarthian productions even before that – for instance, *The Sailor's Progress* (1819) and *The Midshipman's Progress* (1820), both from other people's designs – but they had been inconsequential and purely narrative. *Oliver Twist*, if George had prevailed, might have been another Frank Goodchild. But always there were writers imposing their views: this time Cruikshank would be his own Hogarth even to the extent of publishing the work himself. We first encounter Mr Lambkin (Gent.) having 'come into property' and sallying forth in pursuit of a suitable Lady, blissfully unaware of his own gauche ineptitude. He gets drunk, makes an ass of himself at an evening party, is jilted, falls into bad (theatrical) company, is swindled, falls foul of the law, is laid low by dissipation, attempts all the fashionable cures (hydropathy, trotting, a course of 'new milk'), resolves to mend his ways, begs forgiveness, and is accepted.

As a morality tale Lambkin misses the mark: he is *so* naïve that it is difficult to feel either sympathetic or censorious. He is constantly posing, but so is the society he desperately wants to become a part of – his greatest fault is that he cannot pose as expertly as everyone else. In spite of the realistic settings George has provided for the fall and redemption of his hero – it is the London of whitebait feasts on the river, of musical soirées, promenading in Kensington Gardens, and sepulchral gentlemen's clubs – it is the caricaturist, not the moralist, who wins out. The *Bachelor's Own Book* did not get bad notices – it failed to get noticed at all, and the sales were obviously disappointing enough for George to abandon his projected sequel with a young lady heroine. It was not that the public wasn't ready to be instructed, it was that the artist had omitted to do so: the mannered comedy had obscured the message, and the attempt at moralising had blunted the humour. George did not fall into the same error again. When he returned to Hogarth's model in 1847 it was with a completely different sense of purpose, approach and technique.

Arguably *The Bottle* (1847) could be called George's most successful work, in as much as it achieved its primary objective to reach the mass of the people, and in that it was inalienably the artist's own vision. In eight striking plates *The Bottle* sets out to demonstrate the inexorable consequences of drink, from degradation to crime to ultimate madness. The victims are an ordinary working-man's family and the first step on the path to ruin is an innocent glass of some (unspecified) drink at dinner. The taste acquired, the second plate finds the husband incoherent, his children frightened and their mother pawning their clothes to replenish the bottle. Thereafter the agony is compounded rapidly: the bailiffs move in, the family takes to begging on the streets, the youngest child dies of neglect, violent quarrels break out, in a fit of madness the husband murders his wife, and – in the final plate – is committed to the mad-house.

The message is direct and uncompromising but not without its subtleties, for instance in the way the room itself becomes de-humanised with the disappearance or destruction of its ornaments until it has turned into a cell. The drawing, called coarse by some, is necessarily so from the limitations of glyphography (deliberately chosen to meet the anticipated demand) but is undeniably powerful. George himself had no illusions about it: 'My object was to bring these works out at a price that should be within the reach of the working classes, and [I] therefore sold these eight plates for a shilling and had them produced from my etchings by the only available cheap process at that period,' he wrote later. 'It was a rough process and this accounts for the roughness of the style. When an artist is working for the millions cheapness is the first consideration – but although he may succeed in his object in conveying a lesson, such productions cannot of course be considered as works of art.'*

The public's response on this occasion more than justified his sacrifice. More than 100,000 copies were sold in a few days, it was said: it was exported in shoals as far afield as America and Australia, and dramatised (very suitably) at no less than eight London theatres simultaneously. It was transferred on to lantern-slides, moulded into waxworks, and adapted into a penny-novel. *The Bottle* even inspired Matthew Arnold to compose an ode 'To G. Cruikshank on seeing, in the country, his picture of The Bottle': 'Artist, whose hand, with horror wing'd hath torn from the rank life of towns this leaf. . . .' etc. But while few could deny its impact, there were some who were offended by its implications. Dickens was one of them. On the day after publication he wrote to Forster:

> At Canterbury yesterday I bought George Cruikshank's 'Bottle'. I think it very powerful indeed: the last two plates most admirable. . . . I question whether anybody else living could have done it so well. . . . The philosophy of the thing, as a great lesson, I think all wrong; because, to be striking, and original too, the drinking should have begun in sorrow, or poverty, or ignorance – the three things in which, in its awful aspect, it *does* begin. The design would thus have been a double-handed sword – but too 'radical' for good old George, I suppose.*

Dickens's radical view was one that temperance advocates all too conveniently overlooked: poverty bred drunkenness as often as drinking caused poverty, and it was pointless to denounce the Demon Drink without campaigning, at the same time, against the social conditions that nurtured it. Yet no one knew better than Dickens the personal battle George had had with the bottle, and that in his case it could scarcely be ascribed to 'sorrow, or poverty, or ignorance'.

The posthumous view of George, enshrined in other men's memoirs, inclines to the belief that until he took the pledge he had been a slave to drink all his life. In part this may have been the result of his own enthusiasm for holding himself up as a model convert to the Cause: 'My mother', he once told a temperance audience, 'first lifted the poisoned chalice to my lips' (his eighty-year-old mother, still alive at the time and living under his roof, roundly berated him for this when she came to hear of it). He had been brought up in bibulous times when 'no man was considered a gentleman' – as he put it – 'unless he made his companions drunk', and we know George was no more inhibited than anyone else. But there is no evidence that drink became a serious problem until he was well into middle age.

Henry Vizetelly maintained it started in the early 'forties,* when it was not unknown for George to be taken into police custody in the early hours of the morning 'having been found in the street in an insensible condition', and for his publisher David Bogue to be roused up to bail him out (Bogue did not become Tilt's partner until 1841, nor sole publisher of the *Almanack* until 1844). A friend of Vizetelly's, William Wills, also retailed a pavement episode, in 1846, one night when George had dropped in after dinner: 'The guests departed, leaving the hilarious George with two others to finish the evening; and when the trio got into the street, they found the old difficulty in restraining Cruikshank's boisterous spirits. After trying in vain for something more than an hour to lead him home, they left him – climbing up a lamp-post!'*

So many anecdotes of George's extrovert behaviour – riding home in Dickens's carriage on his head, or grabbing an armful of tablecloths and antimacassars for a costume performance of 'Lord Bateman' – were gleefully passed on that memory seems to have blurred them into one succession of inebriated revels. Even Blanchard Jerrold, who was a boy in the 1840s and 'one of many youngsters who would creep round his chair and endeavour to unravel the mysteries of the extraordinary coiffure', confessed George's visits to his father's house 'were always associated in my mind with late hours and uproarious laughter in the dining-room. Cruikshank was always the last to go.' Dickens at the end of 1842 also commented on this particular habit: 'George Cruikshank got rather drunk here last Friday night,' he wrote to Longfellow, 'and declined to go away until four in the morning, when he went – I don't know where, but certainly not home.'*

And yet George was no Bohemian: his good nature, which in company could be transmuted into over-exuberance, in private displayed itself as kindliness. George Augustus Sala, then an aspiring artist, recalled nervously taking some pen-and-ink sketches up to Myddleton Terrace in 1843 for George's evaluation:

> I can see him now, in a shawl-pattern dressing gown, and with the little spaniel which he has introduced in the meerschaum-smoking reveries in the *Table-Book* basking on the hearth-rug. He received me with great kindness, and kept me with him more than two hours minutely examining my drawings, pointing out their defects, showing (with a little curved gold pencil) how the faults might be remedied, but giving me words of bright comfort and hope. I went away trembling all over with surprise, and gratitude, and joy; but I was yet lingering on the doorstep, when he opened the door and called me back into the passage. These were his 'more last words'. 'It's a very precarious profession,' quoth he, 'and if you mean to do anything you'll have to work much harder than ever the coalheavers do, down Durham Yard.'*

Sala also seems to suggest, paradoxically, that George at this time was an abstainer 'in theory' though by no means in practice; and the aforementioned Wills speaks of the artist, in his pre-*Bottle* days, as flirting with temperance and even turning down dinner-invitations for fear of being led into temptation. The suspicion that Cruikshank was periodically troubled by his own lack of restraint (or that at the very least his wife Mary was) is reinforced by a curious episode which Dickens used to recount.* Early one morning, it seems, George arrived on the doorstep at Devonshire Terrace 'unwashed and smelling of tobacco, beer and sawdust', soliciting breakfast since he had been out all night and was afraid to go home. All Dickens's efforts to persuade him to go home to bed proved useless: he dared, he said, not even think of Islington. But he did consent to go out for a walk, resisting every attempt by his friend to turn their path in the direction of home. The 'walk' lasted all day, punctuated by refreshments and one embarrassing encounter with a close friend of his wife, and was only terminated when sheer exhaustion left no alternative but to return home. To Dickens no doubt this was just another example of old George's idiosyncrasies – otherwise he might have been more discreet – but there was clearly some domestic conflict involved in his drinking, if not some inner conflict as well.

His contemporary drawings on the subject display a marked ambivalence. In 1842, for example, he produced four etchings to accompany John O'Neill's endless poem 'The Drunkard', which included such sobering images as 'The raving maniac and the driveling fool' putting the finishing touches to their alcoholic delirium, and 'The Upas Tree', a nightmarish growth of gin-barrels whose branches drip the stupefying liquor into the glasses of the reeling mob below. Here, you would swear, was an artist never more convinced of the demonic influence of drink, who had seen it destroy his father in middle-age, and who wanted the world to know. But in the very same year George chose to supply the *Comic Almanack* with a caricature of Father Mathew, the Irish apostle of teetotalism whose 1843 crusade on Hampstead Heath had attracted thousands to come forward and sign the pledge. In the cartoon Father Mathew is drawn as a monkish water-pump that has invaded an Englishman's sitting-room and shrilly harangues the family on the wickedness of the home-brewed ale they are about to consume. The gathering is prosperous, hale and hearty, and righteously indignant at this imposition.

These apparently contradictory attitudes in fact reflected real divisions among the drink-reformers themselves, between those who advocated 'temperance' and condemned only the evils of excessive drinking, and those who insisted on total abstinence and a public renunciation of all intoxicating liquor. The actual descriptions of Temperance and Teetotalism had already become irrevocably entangled in the public mind, but within the ranks the debate continued in the early 'forties until the militant abstainers carried the day. That George had long had sympathy with the aims of the moderate reformers is self-evident from his own philippics as far back as *The Gin Shop* (pre-dating the birth of any organised movement in England). But theirs was a comfortable sort of creed, which George was hardly trampling on when he poked fun at a doctrinaire priest (a Catholic into the bargain).

This was the frame of mind in which George approached his message for the millions in *The Bottle.* Since he signed the pledge shortly after its publication, it has inevitably been suggested that he was converted to water-drinking by his own propaganda. It would probably be truer to say he was converted not so much by the message of *The Bottle*, but by the success of *The Bottle*. Whatever its commercial triumph, the most gratifying thing to the artist must have been the critical fanfares of approval acknowledging the plates' power and effect. Even *Punch* (that 'wooden-headed rascal down in Fleet Street' whose head George threatened to knock about when it later twitted him about his temperance zeal) ran a cartoon of a highly disconsolate publican and some fulsome praise of George's etchings:

> The artist has, indeed, shown 'vice its own image'; and he will do as much good as five hundred pledges, or five thousand Temperance Meetings ever achieved. George Cruikshank has exhibited the fatal power of the Bottle-imp; and if Father Mathew deserves a pension of three hundred a year, the artist ought to have at least a thousand for the many benefits he has conferred on the community.*

George's actual conversion to the Cause, according to the Dalziel brothers who claim to have had a first-hand account from the artist himself, was typically impulsive. He had taken the plates for the inspection of Dr Bloomfield, then Bishop of London (or, according to Jerrold's less detailed version, William Cash, chairman of the National Temperance Society), who duly examined them and turned to look Cruikshank full in the face. Was he right in coming to the conclusion that Mr Cruikshank was a staunch total abstainer? George had to admit he did indulge now and again. 'You astonish me, Mr Cruikshank! You very greatly astonish me,' remarked the bishop. 'For how a man who is able to depict so forcibly all the misery, the horror and degradation arising from the indulgence in strong drink, as you have done, and indulge himself is a mystery I cannot understand!' On his way home – George explained to the Dalziels – he felt so inexpressibly ashamed of himself 'that I resolved at once to begin the change which I had long contemplated'.

'It so happened', he went on, 'that a few days after I received an invitation to dine with a gentleman who was famous for the recherché character of his frequent dinner-parties, where the wines were of the choicest brands and most tempting quality. "Now is the time", I said to myself, "to prove my strength of purpose." I was successful in resisting all temptation. The next morning when I went into my study I patted my head and said, "George old boy, you have done well. You have succeeded, George. You have gained a gigantic triumph, and now you must go on unflinchingly and conquer!" And I did.' To emphasise the significance of the moment, the Dalziels wrote, 'the gallant old fellow posed himself in a dramatic attitude, and throwing out his left arm and striking his right hand sharply upon his breast, cried in his ringing voice, FIRE!'*

George liked to invest his irrevocable decisions with an air of theatricality (as he had done in the *Punch* office). Simply to renounce alcoholic beverages was too negative a gesture for one of his temperament: from the moment he decided to forswear drink George was, in effect, committed to the advancement of the Cause. It was a logical enough development. The Temperance Movement may not have lacked for orators, but it certainly was in need of artists: here was a focus not just for his energies, but also for his art – if he could achieve such a massive response with an uncommitted work like *The Bottle*, what could he not achieve with the support of a powerful and proven platform? At the age of fifty-five his horizons were narrowing: the celebrated authors he had once worked with continued to write without his assistance, his own journalistic creations had been virtually still-born. To George, as to many others in the late 1840s, the young Temperance Movement had all the hallmarks of the Establishment of the future. This was the way ahead.

91

7 Nil Desperandum
(1848-1860)

Contrary to many a prediction, the Great Exhibition in Hyde Park did open on time, on 1 May 1851. Paxton's monumental temple of glass and iron did not shatter in fragments the moment the first swarms of shilling-visitors were let loose, nor was the Koh-i-Noor diamond spirited away. On the opening day the Queen graciously shepherded her children past the steam-engines and Egyptian mummies, while outside a traffic-jam of carriages that was to last all summer built up, stretching down Oxford Street and into the heart of the city. All the world was invited to admire Britain's industrial and cultural pre-eminence, and a great part of it came – to be minutely immortalised in George's panorama of the frenetic metropolis for Henry Mayhew's *1851 or The Adventures of Mr and Mrs Sandboys and Family* 'who came up to London to Enjoy Themselves and to see the Great Exhibition'. The splendid occasion was a triumph for the Temperance Movement too, for it had succeeded in getting all alcohol banned from the precincts of the Crystal Palace, much to the disgruntlement of the paying customers who were obliged to wash down their sandwiches with water from the drinking-fountains which *Punch* campaigned to be piped with best bitter. (It was a short-lived triumph, as after the Crystal Palace was removed to Sydenham all George's pamphleteering and furious correspondence with the Archbishop of Canterbury failed to establish the building as a national shrine to teetotalism.)

Britain was approaching her noon of Empire, when nearly one third of the earth's surface would be joyfully (or otherwise) incorporated in her imperial design. The Exhibition stood, at the threshold of a new half-century, as an inspiration for a new generation of manufacturers, soldiers and governors. George Cruikshank's career seemed also to have reached a threshold: for Blanchard Jerrold, George's 'first epoch' came to an end in 1847 with the publication of *The Bottle* and his conversion to the Cause. But the transition was neither so swift or so clear-cut as that implies, and the pattern of life that characterised his declining years – if a man who could still dance the horn-pipe in his eighties can be said to have declined – was moulded by several other events. Certainly by 1851 George had embarked on his muscular phase of teetotalism (he had even thrown away his beloved pipe and inveighed against the weed, too, on every conceivable occasion), but it had not yet come to dominate his work. For several years after 1847 he continued to illustrate fiction, some homely stories by the redoubtable Mrs Gore, a couple of serial novels by now-extinct authors, a translation of *The Pentamerone* (1848) with some fine etchings in his best whimsical virtuoso style, and a fruitful series of collaborations with Henry and Horace Mayhew. The sketches for the Mayhews' various parodies on the traumas of middle-class existence, *The Greatest Plague of Life* (1847) being the adventures of a lady in search of a servant, and *Whom To Marry* (1848) ditto in search of a husband, serve to illustrate just how much George could still have enhanced the pages of *Punch*, if he had not been so intractable.

Indeed, the only significant artistic contribution to the Movement during this period was *The Drunkard's Children* (1848), a sequel to *The Bottle* picking up the fortunes of the only two surviving characters, the son and daughter last seen visiting their demented father in Bedlam. Suggestions for its content poured in on George from all quarters: let it be on the theme of 'the drunkard reclaimed', wrote John Scollier to him.* Another well-wisher proposed that the children should join the Band of Hope and demonstrate the virtues of temperance by making good in the world (as Hogarth's Industrious Apprentice had).

None of this appealed to George, perhaps because he saw no scope there for the development of the 'tragic' theme that had proved so successful with *The Bottle*, or because he was suspicious of happy endings after Mr Lambkin. The result was that both children, in the event, followed their father down the slippery slope by way of the ale-house, she to becoming a prostitute and throwing herself off Waterloo Bridge and he to a life of larceny, transportation and death on board a convict hulk. It was, as Sala pointed out, all slightly ludicrous: 'one reason why the boy thief and girl courtesan look so unconcerned may be that they may be thinking that the "governor" who has cheated the gallows and is now comfortably housed and abundantly fed (there was neither comfort nor food in the drunkard's home) has not made such a very bad thing of it after all'. The logical flaw in George's argument was: if the children – who had been eye-witnesses to the reality of their father's ruin – could not grasp the moral, how could anyone else do better from mere pictorial representation? And the sociological problem remained, as Dickens made clear, deciding now to air the private views he had confided to Forster after *The Bottle*. Drunkenness, he wrote anonymously in *The Examiner*, was not the simple outcome of a casual sip, it had 'a teeming and reproachful history anterior to that stage; and at the remediable evil in that history' – i.e. poverty and deprivation – 'it is the duty of the moralist, if he strikes at all, to strike deep and spare not'.

Predictably *The Drunkard's Children* did not repeat the enormous success of its predecessor. Sequels seldom do, but George, in fact, had a pressing reason for wanting to capitalise on his initial success – he was in debt. In a letter to one of his creditors he gives a full and frank account of his current liabilities, which amount to £1,000, and asks for more time to pay the £334 he owes '. . . but that will be out of my power until I shall have published my new work forming a sequel to *The Bottle*'.* It was a curious moment for him to have been so much out of pocket, even granted the estimate of one of his contemporaries who questioned whether 'his average income, taking the bad years with the good, exceeded six hundred pounds a year'.* The staggering sales of *The Bottle* should have netted George a handsome income for 1847–8, even though he seems to have allowed it to be pirated right, left and centre.

In one of his temperance speeches* – clearly referring to this period – George explained how he 'fell into pecuniary difficulties'. His banker – at that time the private Finsbury Bank: after the debacle he wisely changed to Coutts' – he says, found himself in deep financial trouble and eventually 'blew out his brains'. 1846 had been a disastrous year for bankers and joint stock companies generally, bringing as it did the pay-off for an extraordinary outburst of railway mania at the end of the previous year (when three hundred sets of plans for speculative railway companies had been deposited in Whitehall on a single day). George satirised – perhaps a trifle bitterly? – the nemesis of the wheeler-dealers in 'A Railway Fable' in the 1847 *Comic Almanack*, showing them hot-footing it on to the cross-Channel steamer to escape their creditors. Whether or not this was the cause of his banker's economic tragedy, the fact remained that all George's money had gone with him, 'and I was forced to extricate myself by the most extraordinary exertions'. His friends helped to tide him over for a while, but he insisted that it was only after he had changed his drinking habits that he found the strength of mind to grapple with the problem.

'My fate', he wrote philosophically in the late 1850s, 'has been for the last few years a succession of knock-down blows, or rather throw-backs. But I still fight on.'* The hardest blow of all was the premature death of Mary, his wife. She was only forty-two when she succumbed to one of the major killers in the metropolis, phthisis, a form of tuberculosis. Her death certificate shows she had been suffering from it for at least two years and George himself, in another of his speeches, somewhat cryptically recalled this distressing period – 'a domestic affliction . . . ending in death' – raising the intriguing question of how far Mary's lingering illness was a contributory factor in George's conversion to teetotalism. He certainly believed that all manner of diseases were directly or indirectly caused by alcohol: one friend, he swore, developed symptoms of cholera a few minutes after drinking a glass of beer at his house!

In September 1848 Mary was still well enough, so George wrote to his old friend Alfred Crowquill, 'to express a wish to visit the Surrey Zoological Gardens, and to take me and another little boy with her – I wish to know if you *can* and then I am sure you *will* oblige her'.* But that must have been one of their last excursions: early in January 1849 George is writing to his friend Joseph Gibbs, responding enthusiastically to an invitation to become a godfather: 'Mrs Cruikshank sends her love. She is better certainly, but is still confined to her bed. She will however try to get up next week, when she hopes Mrs Gibbs will come and see her.'* Their optimism was premature. In February, George was obviously at his wits' end, explaining to Crowquill, 'If you will come and see me, I will not only show why I have not made the promised sketch, but also convince you that this – feather-light as it may appear – would if laid on just now break the back of yours truly.'* Mary died on 28 May.

The shock of Mary's death, by his own admission, 'crushed his spirits' and seriously affected his health. If ever there was a stern test of his teetotal convictions it must have been when his own doctor prescribed among other remedies some 'wine to restore his sinking constitution', but George resolutely set his face against it and opted instead for an unpolluted infusion of sea air down at Hythe.*

The marriage had lasted for some twenty-five years, and if virtually the only tribute to Mary that has survived was that 'she threw a charm over the tea and supper tables',* George would not have found that so amiss. For him the paragon of wifely virtues was a woman who had no ambitions beyond the home: his domestic nightmare, as illustrated in the 1847 *Comic Almanack*, would have been to suffer the fate of the wretched husband helplessly surrounded by mewling children and a house going to rack and ruin, while his intense blue-stockinged wife communes with her Muse in the corner. There are many other examples of what would nowadays be described as George's male chauvinism. In 'A New Court of the Queen's Bench' (1850) for the *Comic Almanack* he envisages a court-room entirely manned (if that is the word) by women: the sole male is the defendant being tried for breach of promise. The whole scene is emotionally charged – the jurywomen are sewing, knitting or gossiping, the lady counsel more concerned with their couture and their tea-cups, the court-room itself awash with mirrors and bouquets. In 'The Rights of Women' (1853) he predicts that female enfranchisement would see the emergence of a 'ladies' candidate' offering public dances and canvassing on his good looks. Even if George is here merely reflecting the popular male prejudices of the day, it might also be observed that he was often uncomfortable drawing attractive women: his concept of female beauty was curiously stereotyped and relied a great deal on externals like dress and hair-style. His 'fallen' women often have a lot of character, but his idealised women are faceless and submissive. Any attempt at liberation immediately brands them as frivolous,

95

incompetent or a menace. George's mother, as we know, was a dominating woman but dedicated to her home and family life: it is not too difficult to see in her influence the germ of George's slightly apprehensive view of women, and at the same time his deep-seated need for domestic security.

If any of his friends were surprised when George announced within a few months of Mary's death that he was re-marrying, they might nevertheless have detected in his choice of a new wife a real desire to recreate the kind of domestic refuge he had known in his mother's house and, for a quarter of a century, at Myddleton Terrace. Eliza Widdison was herself a widow, well into her forties, and hardly a stranger. She was the daughter of Charles Baldwyn, who had been George's publisher for several years in the 1820s, a good-looking woman to judge from their Silver Wedding photograph (preserved in the Victoria & Albert Museum). Her 'constant attention and kindness' to George was attested to by close friends of the family. She soon proved a meticulous house-keeper – even down to insisting on signed receipts from the housemaid for her wages* – and a willing secretary when the need arose: her potted biographies of her husband even George found a trifle effusive at times. 'She, for one, fully believed in him', their friend Walter Hamilton wrote after his death, 'and accepted him at his own evaluation, by no means an understated one.'* It was at Eliza's insistence that George would make his periodic stabs at an autobiography; but he never got further than the first few paragraphs. They were married on 7 March 1850, and moved into 48 Mornington Place, a smaller version of the Islington house but equipped with a ready-made studio (it had been his old friend Clarkson Stanfield's home, and the scene of many artistic and theatrical gatherings in earlier years). With them moved George's mother, now unable to walk without her crutch but undimmed in spirit: for her alone was the total ban on alcohol relaxed at Mornington Place, and unrelentingly until her ninetieth year she insisted on her glass of beer at dinner and hot toddy at bedtime! She confirmed George's worst misgivings. 'My poor mother is no more,' he wrote three years later to his godson. 'She was taken ill . . . through drinking some of Cobb's Ale at Margate, and was in bed for six weeks . . . and died on 10th August last.'

In 1851 George was elected vice-president of the newly formed London Temperance League, regarded in water-drinking circles as something of an upstart organisation but which almost at once established a reputation for effective and flamboyant crusading. Its style suited Cruikshank perfectly: he became one of its leading speakers and the moving spirit behind some of its more ambitious, and ultimately abortive, projects, like a deputation to the House of Lords or the construction of a teetotal palace in the Surrey Zoological Gardens (George got as far as designing the building before the trickle of donations finally dried up). His temperance creed was by now fully matured, aggressively teetotal but not yet embracing the doctrinaire principles of the out-and-out prohibitionists, who in the shape of the United Kingdom Alliance were soon lobbying powerfully for a ban on the sale of all intoxicating liquor. George's talent was as a persuader, whether it was demonstrating the moral force of his argument with the etching-needle and paint-brush, or on platforms all over London and as far afield as Bristol and Manchester.

His style of oratory, according to eye-witnesses, was all his own, a singular patchwork of mimicry, histrionics and imposing gravity: the perfect outlet for his pent-up theatrical ardours. His message almost invariably harped back to the theme of *The Bottle*, that drunkenness was the root cause of all society's evils, and crime in particular. 'There are a number of besetting sins connected with drink,' he would inform his audience, 'such as robberies, brutal assaults, garotting, house-breaking, suicide and murder', and having bludgeoned them with this catalogue of vice he would 'challenge the world to produce one single case wherein any real teetotaller has been convicted of one of these crimes. Then, if this be so, what have we to do but to spread this Temperance Movement throughout the length and breadth of the land? And then we should stop, if not all crimes, if not all offences, still the great majority of them.' This edifying insight he would bestow on anyone who would listen, and sometimes anyone who wouldn't. On one occasion (so the story goes) he managed to apprehend a burglar on his premises, summoned the police and on the way to the station delivered a homily to the unfortunate man on the evils of drink, adding that he himself took nothing but water. 'I wish I'd have known that,' grumbled the prisoner. 'I'd have broken your head for you!'

Another important clause in George's temperance manifesto concerned the health-giving and life-prolonging virtues of total abstinence. Rarely would he miss an opportunity to seize upon a glass of water and extend it straight out towards the audience inviting them to contemplate the steadiness of his ageing arm that permitted not a ripple on the water's surface. George Hodder recalled the artist's disarming pride in his own physical fitness: '"Moderation," cried George. "Don't talk to me about moderation – there's no such thing in regard to drink. Give it up entirely as I have done, or it will give you up. Why, look at me, what do you think of that for an arm at seventy-odd years of age," extending his right arm and displaying it, as if about to strike a blow.'* In those days it was a matter of pressing concern to the Movement that many doctors and hospitals, as a matter of course, prescribed a good stiff drink as a recuperative medicine. Increasingly as he got older, George, with his marathon constitutionals over Hampstead Heath, came to be held up as a living testimonial to the superior properties of water.

'Many of us who did not know him at home', wrote Frederick Wedmore 'have at least met him about; for not only was he a familiar figure of the dreary quarter which he inhabited – where the dingy squalor of St Pancras touches on the shabby respectability of Camden Town – but he travelled much in London, and may well have been beheld handing his card to a stranger with whom he had talked casually in a Metropolitan Railway carriage, or announcing his personality to a privileged few who were invited to see in him the convincing proof of the advantages of a union of genius with water-drinking.'* To his personal friends – those with whom he had drunk happily enough only a few years ago – George's newly acquired habit of proselytising at inopportune moments could be infuriating. Each of them dealt with it in his own way. Horace Mayhew found it better to laugh it off when, at a ball in Fitzroy Square, George impetuously interrupted old Joshua Mayhew's toast with the announcement that 'he was a dangerous man . . . every wine-drinker is a dangerous man, sir'. Only a hearty laugh from Horace, and a retort that 'it was only dear old George', saved his father from a bout of apoplexy. And Douglas Jerrold frankly informed his friend that water was, indeed, a very good thing, except on the brain.

Dickens, on the other hand, found it harder to reconcile himself to George's new attitudes. When an embarrassing incident occurred at one of his dinner-parties – George attempted to wrest a glass of wine from one of his guests – Dickens reacted angrily. It was an unpardonable liberty, he exclaimed, adding a veiled reference to George's past, and so disconcerting his friend that he disappeared crestfallen for the rest of the evening. For Dickens the unpredictability of a lovable eccentric was amusing, but not that of a zealot, however lovable. In his way the author tried to warn George of his feelings: in 1848 he wrote to Cruikshank: 'I think the Temperance societies (always remarkable for their indiscretion) are doing a very indiscreet thing in reference to you – and that they will keep many of your friends away from your side, when they would most desire to stand there.'* When George had first told Dickens at a luncheon party that 'a man had better take a glass of prussic acid than fall into the other habit of taking brandy-and-water', his friend had jovially put it down as one of George's quirks, and agreed with him. But the months, years, rolled by and temperance had become a way of life, alienating him inexorably from his old friends.

George felt this deeply. In April 1851 he wrote to Dickens complaining of his 'coolness', wondering why they had not met for so long. Dickens responded with assurances 'that I have never felt the slightest coolness towards you, or regarded you with any other than my old unvarying feeling of affectionate friendship'. Circumstances, he said, had prevented their meeting but very soon he would come to see George and 'with one shake of the hand dispel any lingering remainder, if any there be, of your distrust'.* If Dickens could have dissociated George from his convictions, doubtless they would have remained friends; but their friendship could not survive his growing distaste for the fanatical aspect of the whole Temperance Movement, their 'whole-hoggery' as he put it in a philippic entitled 'Whole Hogs' in his magazine *Household Words* in August 1851. He attacked their 'intemperate assumption of infallibility' and protested at their implied criticism of moderate drinkers: 'Society won't come in and sign the pledge. Therefore Society is fond of drunkenness, sees no harm in it, favours it very much, *is* a drunkard. . . .'

Clearly he detected symptoms of this ailment in his friend; but what seems to have distressed him most was the content of George's *Fairy Library*, the first volume of which was published in 1853 and which for Dickens epitomised a herd of whole hogs on the rampage. The *Fairy Library* was intended, at the outset, to contain the whole canon of nursery stories illustrated – and edited – by Cruikshank. By 'editing', however, George meant re-writing, so as to exclude all the morally reprehensible parts and to insert what might be called wholesome precepts. The first of the Library, *Hop-o'-my-Thumb*, was accordingly pruned of the ogre's worst excesses and infiltrated with models of juvenile virtue, washing with cold water and going to bed early without complaining. Even more significantly the whole tale was organised to demonstrate the evils of drink (the poverty of Hop's family) and the benefits flowing from abstinence (in the newly teetotal, ogre-free kingdom). The etchings are harmless and delightful, but the text is unashamedly a temperance tract for children.

George must have nurtured this project ever since Thackeray had written his generous article in 1840. 'May Jack the Giant Killer, may Tom Thumb, may Puss in Boots be one day revivified by his pencil. Is not Whittington sitting yet on Highgate Hill, and poor Cinderella still pining in her chimney nook? . . . We pray Mr Cruikshank to remember them.' And indeed four out of five of Thackeray's suggestions became subjects of the *Fairy Library*.

The project was the last straw for Dickens: it was trespassing on a sacred preserve of fancy, romance and imagination, a 'fairy flower-garden' trampled on by a whole hog rooting among the roses. In 'Frauds on the Fairies' (*Household Words*, October 1853) he reproached the artist for his 'means of propagating the doctrines of Total Abstinence, Prohibition of the Sale of Spirituous Liquors, Free Trade, and Popular Education. For the introduction of these topics, he has altered the text of a fairy story; and against his right to do any such thing we protest with all our might and main.' Dickens went on to imagine all kinds of further horrors being perpetrated, like a vegetarian version of Robinson Crusoe, and Cinderella starting life as a star of the Band of Hope and ending up a totalitarian tyrant.

George may have touched a nerve in Dickens's creative system by his treatment of the fairies, but the author's criticisms were a direct body-blow to George. Cuthbert Bede visited Mornington Place shortly after their publication and reported him to be 'smarting from the effects of Dickens's article'. Nevertheless, he refused to relent and published the next two stories, *Jack and the Beanstalk* and *Cindrella* (1854), with a similar infusion of cautionary ethics. But then the series came to a sudden and premature end: a fourth fable, *Puss in Boots*, was started but was not published for another ten years. As he explained later to a well-wisher, George despaired of swimming against a current of hostile criticism and public disinterest, engendered (as he saw it) by Dickens:

> Such testimonials, I assure you [he wrote in response to a letter of support] repay me in one way, for many days of severe and anxious toil – that meets with little more reward and encouragement than this agreeable knowledge, of having amused and perhaps instructed the child in a way that meets with the entire approbation of the parent. But to rewrite these fairy tales so as to get rid of everything that might be objectionable – to give indeed a new character to the story – and at the same time to preserve all the good and extraordinary parts of the original, together with the production of the illustrations upon steel, I have found to be a work taking up a considerable portion of time – and the sale of the work has not been sufficient remuneration to induce me to proceed. Mr Bogue the Publisher as well as myself expected that these books would have had a large sale – but Mr Charles Dickens thought proper to write a very severe, and as I conceive uncalled-for, condemnatory criticism upon the first number, which was repeated by other critics and raised a prejudice against these trifles – and checked the sale – most persons supposing from what he stated that the book was unfit for the use of children.*

George was never a man to flinch from open confrontation in defence of his interests, nor did he on this occasion. In February of 1854 (see below) he penned an open letter from *Hop-o'-my-Thumb to Charles Dickens Esq.*, engaging this literary giant as boldly as he had the ogre. His editor, wrote the wee mite, had failed to see any mercy in a man who would leave his children to perish in a forest and had 'felt certain that any father acting in such a manner must either be mad or under the influence of intoxicating liquor, which is much the same thing. . . .' Moreover:

> To insist upon preserving the entire integrity of a fairy tale, which has been and is constantly altering in the recitals, and in the printing of various editions in different countries, appears to my little mind like shearing one of your own 'whole hogs' where there is 'great cry and little wool'.

The tone of the letter was good-humoured, ending with a woodcut of Hop driving a flock of well-fattened hogs back to *Household Words*. But as the fate of the *Fairy Library* became sealed, the tone of Hop's letter in its subsequent reprints grows less genial, omitting the more flattering references to Dickens. The friendship had finally foundered on an ideological reef.

1854 was a cruel year for George's publisher, David Bogue, too. For thirteen years – ever since old Charles Tilt had invited him, the youngest of his clerks, out of the blue to become his partner and successor – Bogue had been George's friend and ally, displaying an undentable faith in the artist's powers, and being rewarded by some notable successes like *The Bottle*, *Mr & Mrs Sandboys* and the early issues of the *Comic Almanack*. But by 1853 the old *Almanack* had clearly outlived its inspiration, and was quietly put to rest. Yet neither that, nor the disappointing reaction to the first of the *Fairy Library* could persuade Bogue that George's public was not still at large, or that the artist – whose etching skills had in no way diminished – could not be re-launched on a whole new generation.

Bogue's plan was for *George Cruikshank's Magazine*, a showcase for all the formidable skills the artist had amassed in his long career. It was to be edited by Frank Smedley, a wheel-chair-bound writer of stirring fiction (Smedley recalled his first interview with George: 'Good God,' cried George in amazement at seeing the crippled author, 'I thought you galloped round on horses!'), but in practice the style, humour, contributors, the overall direction, were to be George's. A make-or-break endeavour to re-establish his reputation. George responded with a will, producing for the first number (January 1854) an epic frontispiece, 'Passing Events or The Tail of the Comet of 1853' in which whole Russian armies, Chinese bannermen, fleets, governments, temperance demonstrations, cattle shows, and curiosities of the London season (the ceiling-walker, the bulls from Layard's excavations at Nineveh, the strange ant-eater on display at the Zoo) all jostle for recognition within the space of a few square inches. It is a blockbuster of an etching, and even if its total impact is marred by over-elaboration it repays detailed investigation – even the whole hogs get a mention.

Sadly, *George Cruikshank's Magazine* made only two appearances. It offered the public nothing new, unless it was an insight into George's newest preoccupations – like 'Tobacco Leaves' a fulmination in several panels against the narcotic weed. Cuthbert Bede relates how he was summoned to Mornington Place, in the preparatory stages of the magazine, and invited to write the text for an article exposing a 'hideous, abominable, and most dangerous custom' which George was determined to try to put down. It was an evil 'patent to everyone, both indoors and out of doors, in the streets and railway carriages, and omnibuses and all public vehicles . . . not confined to the young or old, it was most injurious in its effects, and it only required the public attention to be pointedly directed to it to have it stopped and put down'. Bede waited apprehensively to learn what this horror was, that was tearing the moral fabric of the country to shreds: it was nothing less, George announced, than the habit of the population 'of placing the handles of their sticks, canes, parasols or umbrellas to their mouths, and either sucking them or tapping their teeth with them!'

It is tempting to think that George in his later years was often more satirical, or mischievous, than his contemporaries gave him credit for. And yet as George enlarges on his project the doubts creep in. Once it had appeared in *George Cruikshank's Magazine*, the article was going to be reprinted in the form of a pamphlet, which would be distributed free to the public, posted outside railways stations, and tossed into omnibuses as they passed by! And very likely it would have been (for George was an ardent pamphleteer) and enjoyed as a joke by the travelling public. That was the trouble with having been a humorist now turned reformer – one could never tell if his jokes were obsessive, or his real obsession laughable.

The death of the magazine was yet another of George's massive 'knockdown blows'. First he had lost his money, then his wife: his brother Robert was now seriously ill, 'fallen away to a shadow', as George explained to his godson (he finally succumbed to the lingering bronchitis in March 1856). And now dawned the realisation that he had lost his public too. His first instinct was to blame the magazine's collapse on Bogue and Smedley who had, he wrote crossly, 'completely ruined it from the outset', for it was an unpalatable fact – and one which he was to be reminded of ten years later – that George was now one of the old school, no longer a name guaranteed to sell. New stars were rising in his chosen field, men with a modern approach like John Tenniel and Charles Keene; and soon book illustration would be dominated by a new generation of artists, Millais, Rossetti and others, more polished and sophisticated, perhaps, even if no better visualisers of character than their predecessors. It is a desperate experience, growing out of fashion; and the temptation to dazzle with effects, as in 'Passing Events', was strong but ultimately self-defeating.

As it happened, George only fully illustrated one more book, and that was Brough's *Life of Sir John Falstaff* (1858), a subject well-suited to the artist's best historical style. For the rest the only commissions that came along were for title-pages, frontispieces, the odd woodcut, or charitable 'guest appearances' for the privately produced books of friends. David Bogue's firm was taken over shortly after the collapse of the magazine, and other publishers became increasingly reluctant to contemplate George's services. Who knew what teetotal sermons they might get for their money? For a couple of years the periodicals, those voracious devourers of material, offered the prospect of piecemeal employment – some woodcuts for *Cassell's Illustrated,* whose publisher, John Cassell, was George's fellow vice-president in the London Temperance League, for *The British Workman,* a serial for *Sharpe's London Magazine,* and for *The Illustrated London News* a grand panorama of a temperance rally in Sadlers Wells (May 1854) with George as the central figure, ushering excited converts on to the stage to sign the pledge.

This poorly paid hack work painfully served to underline, if nothing else, the inferior status of an illustrator amongst artists. In everything he did, an illustrator, to George's mind, was the slave of his publishers: they it was who had always stood between him and a fortune, always managed to 'swallow the oyster and leave him the shells', as he put it. And yet his own enterprises as a publisher had not brought him that fortune either. If he had to begin his career over again, George once told William Bates in conversation, it would be with the painting-brush and not the etching-needle: then all publishers and their breed could go to the devil. As it was, even the humblest painter of average competence could safely hope to earn as much, or more, than him.

That George would have made a painter (as he would have made an admiral or an actor had circumstances demanded) he was in no doubt. Lockhart had intimated as much thirty years ago, the celebrated Clarkson Stanfield had positively encouraged him to take up the brush, and only pressures of work had prevented him from capitalising on his one success in 1830 (when the Royal Academy had accepted an oil-painting for its Summer Exhibition). It is true he felt the lack of any academic training very keenly, and his first sight of Raphael's cartoons made him even more acutely conscious of his own shortcomings. But these were technical deficiencies which even at the age of sixty were, surely, not irremediable? In April 1853 George retraced his steps to the Royal Academy, enrolled as the student he should have become when he was twelve, and carried his pencil and sketch-pad into the Antique class to study the classical torsos. But for one who had been drawing from his observations of real life for over fifty years, the minute analysis of lumps of stone failed to fire his imagination. The course went on without him.

George was undaunted. Cuthbert Bede, visiting his studio later that year, saw dozens of oil-paintings in various stages of completion: indeed, one or two had already hung at the Academy, like 'Tam o'Shanter' (1852) based on Burns's poem of a flight from the witches, and another foray into the supernatural, the meeting of Oberon and Titania in 'A Midsummer Night's Dream' (1853). In subject-matter George's oils were very much an extension of his etchings (at first) – painted visions of fairyland such as 'Cindrella' (1854) or else humorous set-pieces like 'A Runaway Knock' (1855) in which an entire household has been aroused from its slumbers by fugitive urchins knocking at the door. A similarly skittish little subject, 'Disturbing the Congregation' (1855), caught the fancy of Prince Albert when it was exhibited at the British Institution and – apparently deemed not too frivolous – was purchased for the royal collection.

But the same temptations that were now visible in his etchings, that were to create miniature epics, also afflicted his paintings. The Dalziels told a story, probably apocryphal and certainly inaccurate, but which illustrated George's ambitions perfectly:

> On the occasion of his exhibiting a small oil painting called The Dropped Penny [in fact it was called 'Disturbing the Congregation'] the fact that it was purchased by Prince Albert no doubt called extra special attention to it. One gentleman was most anxious to have it, or if this was impossible, would he make a replica? This George declined to do but undertook a commission, only on the understanding that choice of subject and of size were to be left to him. This was readily agreed to. The Dropped Penny was a little thing 18 × 24 inches. It was a comic picture – two urchins in church, one of whom having dropped a penny on the stone floor is about to pick it up, but they are observed by the beadle. When the new work was completed the gentleman was invited to see it. He found, to his amazement, a picture 16 × 20 feet, subject, The Raising of Lazarus. George always thought his true forte was the Grand Historical.*

There is no record of even George having painted a picture of such dimensions: all the same, friends spoke reliably of some pretty massive canvases to be seen at Mornington Place – one of them embracing the entire battle of Agincourt; another, 'Christ Riding into Jerusalem', remained unfinished to the end of his days. The father of them all, 'The Worship of Bacchus', measured over 13 feet by 7 feet 8 inches.

The critics of the day, for the most part, did not vote George's paintings a great success. They found the style crude, the tones and colours unsubtle, but they admitted the humour and vigour – particularly of his anecdotal and less presumptuous works. All the familiar skills of his etching, his grouping and characterisation, he brought to the easel but he was never entirely at ease with a paint-brush in his hand. The etcher's touch remained with him, the concrete sensation (he explained to a friend) of graver on steel so engrained in his fingers that he could not rid himself of it. His awareness of these shortcomings tempered, though it never dashed, his ultimate self-confidence in his ability as a painter. 'I have *just* finished a picture which I am just going to take to the Royal Academy,' he told Pulford in 1854. 'It is more like a picture than anything I have ever done – and everyone who has seen it pronounces it to be my *best*. You would be surprised at my improvement in oil, as indeed I am myself. I have got several commissions for pictures and so I shall dash on. . . .'*

These commissions were by now the mainstay of his income, as the offers for illustrations fell away. The most George got for a private painting, Jerrold records, was £800 for 'The Fairy Ring' (1855), paid by a gentleman from Preston. But that must have been exceptional: a receipt for 'The Runaway Knock' shows that it was sold to Joseph Robinson for £100 (frame included) in the same year, and George's own estimate of his smaller works was even more modest. Haggling over price with an unnamed patron, he wrote later: 'I shall be much disappointed unless I get that sum for this favourite work of mine, and in order to make the matter satisfactory to you, if you send me a cheque for that sum I will paint you a small picture which I shall consider worth 20 or 25 pounds. . . .' When there were no commissions George painted on regardless, sending out invitations to likely customers for private views in his own studio. When all else failed he ransacked his imagination for any other means to deploy his pencil profitably. He designed, unbidden, a new cap for the Infantry, only to be informed by the Army that it had no intention of changing its current headwear. He was then fired with enthusiasm for a new stove invented by an old friend and known as the Sheringham Ventilator: he drew sketches of it, had a prototype installed in his own draught-ridden studio, and endorsed it with relish to anyone who would listen ('almost entire absence of any deposit of soot at the back of the chimney . . . strong draught and perfect combustion').

But his most high-flown and spectacular project took shape in 1856 after the end of the Crimean War – no less than the building of a national railroad for Turkey! Oblivious to the impenetrable morass of Ottoman bureaucracy, George drew up plans with his friend Joseph Gibbs, a civil engineer, prepared a handwritten prospectus, and besieged Sir Austen Henry Layard for his support. That gentleman, long famed for his great excavations in Asia Minor, was now a Junior Minister, diplomat and acknowledged Turkophile – an essential ally in any British undertaking in Constantinople. George emerged from an interview with Layard in July 1856 convinced that he had sold the whole enterprise to him, and that Layard would return from his winter tour of Turkey with a government concession in his briefcase. In February George wrote to Layard reminding him of their supposed agreement, of the minor alterations the M.P. had suggested, of the prospectus he had taken to Turkey, and hoping that 'you would fill the position of Chairman to the proposed company', and as he was also Chairman of the Ottoman Bank 'you would kindly interest the directors and management of that establishment in our favour . . . and I have now to hope that when Mr Gibbs and myself have the pleasure of an interview that everything will be arranged in a satisfactory manner to all parties'.* Layard's reply must have come, therefore, as a thunderbolt: the Ottoman Bank, he wrote, already had a proposal for a railway before the government, George was suffering a 'complete misconception as to what passed last summer' and he had no intention of connecting himself personally with Mr Gibbs's scheme. Layard, who was a leading subscriber to George's testimonial ten years later, clearly had more regard for him as an artist than as a business man.

Quite how George could have contemplated any involvement with the Sick Man of Europe, when there were so many casualties knocking on his own door by this time, is hard to fathom. His papers dating from the mid-fifties show him totally immersed in his temperance crusading, organising processions, laying foundation stones, addressing working-men's clubs, public meetings and teetotal dinners. And as his reputation within the Movement grew, so did the torrent of pitiful letters begging either his help or his money that arrived through his letterbox. Seemingly incapable of turning down any deserving plea, he could (and did) find himself 'reclaiming' up to half a dozen 'most dreadful cases' at one time. Of his success rate there is no record but even the backsliders, like the one-time journalist John Daniell, often returned to George in their hour of need. Among the more fluent of George's derelict correspondents, Daniell wrote:

> Had I followed your advice 11 years ago, I would not be now as I am, neither need I come to any man's door. . . . But I fell in with the accursed habit of drink, lost my own self-respect, so that in coming to you today I have only to appeal to your *mercy* and not to your justice. The vicissitudes of literary life have lately pressed hard on me. . . . I solemnly assure you that I was unable to buy a meal of food yesterday or today as yet, and I appeal to your scholarly sympathies and personal generosity for a little help to assist me just slightly for a day or two. I shall call in an hour for such answer as you may deign to accord me.*

That George was possibly almost as hard up as he was probably did not occur to him: George's friends ascribed the insolvency of his latter years to his own reckless philanthropy. There may have been another, more private, reason, though few of them knew about it.

8 *Memorials*
(1860-1878)

To his obituary-writers George's personal life presented a perplexing problem. Most of them – although a generation removed from the old gentleman – knew of his youthful reputation from hearsay and had seen the earthiest of his Regency satires in some collector's portfolio (or at the great exhibition of his life work at the Westminster Aquarium). And yet at the same time they were confronted with the evidence of their own eyes, of a man who for thirty years past had spoken out fearlessly against the prevailing vices of the day, drunkenness and smoking, betting shops and inhumanity to children. Some of them, trying to reconcile the disparities, spoke of George 'atoning for' and 'making amends' for his earlier life-style: others even went so far as to suggest he had been misunderstood, that he had always been fired with reforming zeal but that the spirit of those far-off, disreputable times had militated against him – why, had he not since actually apologised for ridiculing the Prince Regent? Others, taking sanctuary in the stout Victorian principle of *de mortuis nihil nisi bonum*, wrote exclusively about his work, like Frederick Wedmore who explained somewhat enigmatically: 'nothing is less truthful than biography; or rather nothing is more one-sided. The admiring acquaintance . . . the enthusiastic relative – these, you know, are hardly the persons to whom the world must go at last for the veracious and balanced story. Possibly it is never forthcoming . . . to each will have been afforded the means of telling us something; by each much will necessarily be witheld, and much unknown.'

There was indeed a select group of 'admiring acquaintances' for whom the dilemma was particularly horned. For they knew of – or at least suspected – an aspect of George's life that was utterly at odds with the authorised version of the rest of his life. William Bates and Walter Hamilton, both of whom wrote long panegyrics to George after his death, certainly were aware of a 'skeleton in the house' and corresponded anxiously with each other as to how the matter should be treated. Others, they admitted, had hinted at the facts, but for themselves resolved to close ranks so that 'his memory be kept clean by his works – they at least are innocent'.* Another friend, S. C. Hall, wrote to Bates in due course approving of his discreet course of action: 'You have taken a generous and, I believe, a just view of poor George. Who is he that will cast the first stone? Who are those that judgeth another? I am thankful that there is no Asmodeus to take the roof off my house – and "look in". How few are there who could bear that process?'*

The skeleton, it transpires, was one that not a few eminent Victorians buried in their time: it seems that George, for the greater part of his second marriage, was living a double life – one of routine domesticity with Eliza at Mornington Place, the other round the corner, where he kept a mistress and raised a whole brood of children. Ironically, it is the letter from Hamilton, who was so concerned with George's reputation, that has offered the clearest clue to the mystery, since it mentions in a reproachful tone the provisions of George's will.

It is certainly a fascinating document. In it 'to my dear and beloved wife Eliza' George left the sum of £50, all plate, linen, china, glass, furniture and household effects, together with £100 worth of his etchings. He adds that she was otherwise provided for (and, indeed, mentions elsewhere that all his investments in the Temperance Land Society were in his wife's name). The income from all the rest of his personal estate was to go to 'Adelaide Archibold (otherwise Adelaide Altree)' and ultimately to her ten children, who are specified by name. They are: George Robert, Adelaide, William Henry, Albert Edward, Alfred Hills, Eliza Jane, Ada Rose, Emma Caroline, Nelli Maude, and Arthur Altree Archibold. Searches at the General Register Office in London suggest that they were born in the Camden district between the years 1858 and 1875 (when George himself was between the ages of sixty-six and eighty-three), and a sample selection of their birth certificates gives the name of their father as 'George Archibold' and his profession as 'artist'. In each case the address is 31 Augustus Street, Regent's Park.

George's will also reveals a little about the nature of his relationship with Adelaide: in it he bequeaths to her 'all such furniture, books, wines, and household effects belonging to me as shall at the time of my death be in the said house, 31 Augusta (sic) Street, or in any other house in which she may then be living'. The fact that they were there in sufficient quantity to be specified in a separate clause seems to indicate that George had virtually set up a second home at Augustus Street. (And the wines – what are we to make of them? They are an unusual choice of investment for a teetotaller, and if the remnants of his pre-Temperance cellar, must have been rare vintages indeed.)

Hamilton suggests it was possible that Eliza knew of her husband's other life, yet also insists (without offering any personal evidence) that she was amazed at the contents of the will. It would be astonishing if she had lived with George for over twenty years and had no inkling of the circumstances. The Archibold house, after all, was not in some circumspect corner of St John's Wood – it was in the same neighbourhood as Mornington Place, five minutes' walk away across the railway line.

Even when George and Eliza moved from Mornington Place in 1865, it was only to 263 Hampstead Road – still less than ten minutes' walk for one of George's vibrant constitution.

That does not leave the impression that George expected, or wished, to conduct a furtive affair: and honesty (we have it in his own hand) was the virtue he prized above all others. If Eliza in fact knew of the house across the railway line perhaps she recognised and, for reasons of her own, bowed to an inordinate need on George's part. He was passionately fond of children, yet was fated to two childless marriages. He was a highly popular godfather, with a string of godchildren whose middle name was Cruikshank, and nothing moved him more deeply than the sight of children deprived or exploited. He was a staunch advocate (in his tract *A Slice of Bread and Butter* (1857)) of compulsory state education for every child long before it became an accomplished fact with Foster's Act of 1871, and George's very last political print, 'Our Gutter Children', a glass-etching published in 1869 at his own expense, was a counterblast against a much-publicised proposal to 'export' waifs and strays to America.

It might be argued that George's other family was a form of indulgence on his part, which ill-became a man who preached so vehemently against other forms of indulgence. But his morality was of an exclusively secular, utilitarian nature – aimed at creating a happier, more equitable society. To George a course of action was to be judged not by whether it was sinful, but whether it was harmful. ('There is no other process by which we are to judge ourselves,' he once told his fellow-abstainers, 'or by which our opponents ought to judge us. Let them show us the *harm* we either do now or are likely to do ultimately. . . .'*) Although he professed himself to be 'a humble protestant', that was really to emphasise his inherited aversion to the rites of Rome ('a very good religion for candle-makers and wax chandlers and candlestick-makers'*): his interest in the established Church extended mainly to what social good it could achieve. His drinking, he would have submitted, could have done harm to society, but his personal relationships could not. But whether he ever considered the potential harm to his wife or the children or himself, we may never know.

On one thing all George's acquaintances agreed – that the energy and enterprise of his old age were quite phenomenal. At a moment when most men would have been contemplating retirement, George not only embarked on a new and demanding relationship, immersed himself in temperance affairs and launched into a new career as a painter, he also (on the verge of seventy) took up command of a new Volunteer Corps. The 24th Surrey Rifle Volunteers, otherwise known as the Havelocks, was born at a public meeting of abstainers in December 1860. Two months later George offered his services as an adjutant, only to find himself (perhaps as the only man with volunteer experience, albeit that in the days of the musket) appointed commander of the corps by the War Office, with the rank of Lieutenant-Colonel. The men soon discovered that George had lost none of his adolescent enthusiasm for uniforms and inspections, rifle-drill and field-days – indeed, they would complain 'his zeal was of more than an ordinary character' – but the administration of the Havelocks was bedevilled from the start.

The War Office, allocating equipment for one battalion, discovered that the teetotallers had recruited nearly four battalions; then the Lord Lieutenant of Kent complained that the Surrey men had been recruiting in his county, and ordered them to stop forthwith. Since this effectively halved the Havelocks's catchment area, Whitehall advised George to move to Middlesex instead: so it was that, a year after their formation, the corps began life afresh, with headquarters in Lincoln's Inn, as the 48th Middlesex Rifle Volunteers. By the end of 1862 the records show numbers falling off alarmingly, because of the expense of buying the uniforms, and because of murmurings within the ranks against the commander. An unruly meeting in February 1863 led to the suspension of a Major Sanders and an Ensign Woodward for insolence and insubordination to Lieutenant-Colonel Cruikshank, nearly provoking a mutiny, as George explained in his report to the Lord Lieutenant:

> I have to inform your Lordship that the acting adjutant has reported to me that Major Sanders and Ensign Woodward attended one of the drill-grounds not in uniform, and that Major Sanders did then and there address the men on the subject of his suspension, thus endeavouring to excite the sympathies of the men in his favour and against myself. . . .*

Letters of apology smoothed that particular unpleasantness over – though not George's pride – but the same culprits were behind a much more serious attack on George's authority a few years later. In the summer of 1868 they and a group of other officers ('mean and contemptible conspirators endangering the very existence of the corps', as George described them) presented a memorandum to the Lord Lieutenant, to the effect that they considered George too old to fulfil his duties as commanding officer. The Havelocks were split down the middle, other officers siding with George: 'You have been treated with the blackest ingratitude', Captain Hurley assured him, 'by a set of men not fit to black your boots . . . . The weapons that these men have used would have soiled the hands of the veriest wretch God ever let crawl in infamy upon this earth.'*

The complaint, reaching the War Office, only resulted in the cashiering of the rebels, but now George resolved to resign with as much dignity as he could muster, and a hoped-for honorary colonelcy in recognition of his eight years' service. Yet once again fate slipped him a sharp uppercut: the Army considered George was presuming too much. The Duke of Wellington accepted his resignation, but found he 'had reason for doubting that I can recommend you as an Honorary Colonel, and I lose no time in informing you'.* The reason was explained in due course:

> The Duke has received a list of Honorary Colonels in Middlesex and finds that they are all Field Marshals or Generals except five. Of these five, one is Governor General of India, one commands a regiment of militia, two are peers, and one is Col. McMurdo. Colonel Cruikshank will thus see that he is quite out of the category and cannot with propriety be recommended as Honorary Colonel.*

Some of his more faithful colleagues proposed to make an appeal to the Duke, but George firmly rejected the idea. So ended his military career (that had stretched, one could almost say, from before Trafalgar almost until the Franco-Prussian War), not in a blaze of glory, but at least with the consolation of a fellow-officer who wrote: '. . . if you had one fault (excuse me for saying so) it was that you were too kind and too lenient!'

A yellowing photograph of George, a little uncomfortable but resplendent in his dress-uniform of the Havelocks, might explain why his subordinates in the corps formed such conflicting views of him. It confirms a pen-portrait, quoted by Jerrold, of the artist in his riper years: 'slightly below the middle height, spare but solid of frame, somewhat long-armed and short-legged as powerful and long-lived men are apt to be . . . a prominent aquiline nose that Caesar would have liked to look upon, and a mouth cut in firm, sharp lines and from whose corners grew an ambiguous pair of hirsute ornaments which were neither moustaches, nor whiskers, nor beard but partook vaguely of the characteristics of all three'. Behind that patriarchal foliage could easily have lurked a formidable presence: only closer inspection would have revealed the 'blue-grey eyes full of a cheerful, sparkling light'. Even if he did not always bestow it on his rifle-volunteers, George retained his buoyant good humour to his last days – such at least was Sala's abiding memory of him:

> And then he shook his head in the oracular manner so distinctive of him, and departed, waving his celebrated gingham umbrella. . . . I never knew a man who made such effective exits as did George Cruikshank; and it is (as all actors know) an extremely difficult thing to quit the stage with éclat. When George left you with a flourish of the umbrella, or a snapping of the

fingers (or sometimes with a few steps of the hornpipe or the Highland fling), he never failed to extort from you a round of mental applause, and you felt yourself saying, watching his rapidly departing form . . . 'God bless the dear old boy! How well he looks and what spirits he has.'*

'Nil desperandum' was his avowed motto:* whatever life threw up at him, he knew he would find himself 'at it again'. And nothing in his whole career made such calls on this fund of resilience as the years of labour, love and ultimate disappointment expended on his titanic painting 'The Worship of Bacchus'. The great work was begun at the end of 1860 and monopolised his energies for three years. It was to be his life-statement, a mind-shattering exposé of the myths of drinking that would penetrate to and stir the consciences of every section of society. It would stand – all one hundred square feet of it – as an object lesson for generations as yet unborn, who would come to look at it, see themselves there and go away fortified against the devils of hard liquor.

Such an undertaking needed capital, of course, which George conspicuously lacked. But supremely confident of its commercial potential, he assumed all financial responsibility for the project, but to see him through the long months of actual creation a committee of sponsors was formed who advanced him what was prudently called 'spending-money'. There were plenty of men prepared to share his optimism – by no means all of them abstainers – and an arrangement was made whereby George would first complete his design in a watercolour sketch, from which a steel-engraving would be prepared. The sale of these prints would not only repay the investors, they would cover all expenses of the great oil-painting itself. That was the theory. In practice George was so eager to translate his vision on to canvas that he quite neglected the engraving. All through 1862 he toiled at the masterpiece, adding rank upon rank of worshippers at the wine-god's altar until they covered the painting in their hundreds.

'I have not the vanity to call it a picture,' he explained in the lecture which was intended to accompany the finished painting. A 'map' was his description, a series of pictorial diagrams surrounding the central figures of Bacchus himself and his sinister followers Silenus and the Bacchantes. Every stage of life was represented, from the cradle (a mother weaning her baby on gin) to the death-bed (a doctor prescribing port for the dying), and every station in life. There is the duchess sipping her wine, and the gentry on their hunters downing their stirrup-cups: there are undergraduates supping Trinity Ale ('the strongest, I believe, that is brewed in the whole country'), haymakers carousing, soldiers in a drunken brawl, and wedding-guests drinking a health to the bride. Freemasons and civic dignitaries, policemen and publicans – none of them are spared, not even the clergyman refreshing himself in the vestry on the quiet, or the missionary attempting to seduce a Mohammedan (the only one who seems to emerge unscathed) with a bottle of spirits. By the time George had finished his *magnum opus* his sponsors had paid him more than a thousand pounds.

The fruits of Cruikshank's prodigious effort were unveiled to the world, in November 1862, at a small gallery in Wellington Street off the Strand. The loyal committee came and toasted its success in tea, then waited for the public to come flocking in. But the public didn't flock in. 'The Worship of Bacchus' was moved to a more suitable site in Exeter Hall and, as an added inducement, supplemented by an impressive retrospective collection of George's work. Soirées were held, and a daily lecture by the artist advertised. Thackeray came, was overcome by waves of nostalgia for the Cruikshank of his youth, and wrote a generous article in *The Times*. But still the public's curiosity was unawakened. Blanchard Jerrold recalled his visit and finding the room in Exeter Hall deserted, except for George who greeted him with 'a wild, anxious look in his face' and who continually glanced at the door whenever he heard approaching footsteps. It reminded him, Jerrold said, of that other exhibition room where Haydon had stood solitary and broken-hearted among his disregarded paintings.

But George shouldered his burden of disappointment with more resolution. He remembered the royal favour he had once enjoyed with Prince Albert: he was dead now, but perhaps the Queen might remember him as one of her husband's favourite artists. Hopefully he sent off to the Palace a typically Cruikshankian appeal via Sir Charles Phipps:

> For the last 18 years I have been advocating the cause of Temperance at a very great sacrifice of time, but I have struggled on and persevered, believing that I was labouring for the benefit of the working classes. My last effort in this cause is the large picture of 'The Worship of Bacchus' now exhibiting at Exeter Hall. I have produced this work in the hope that it may assist in checking the tide of intemperance. It has been exhibiting in London for some time and it is intended shortly to send it round to the principal towns with a lecturer, and my object in now troubling you is to ask if you think it possible that Her Majesty would graciously condescend to view this picture provided it were removed for this purpose to one of the royal palaces. . . . I may say that the mere fact of Her Majesty having been graciously pleased to view this picture would not only give the work great interest in the metropolis but would do so likewise in every part of Her Majesty's dominions wherever it might be exhibited, and I firmly believe that such patronage would under the blessing of God produce the most beneficial results upon the working part of the population. I know I am

asking very much, but I feel assured you will believe me to be one of the last persons who would intrude upon those sacred feelings which now occupy Her Majesty's mind. . . .*

And so on. The 'sacred feelings' occupying Victoria at that time were of course her prolonged leave-taking of Albert, who had been dead these two years, which had prevented her from fulfilling any public duty. So it was quite a triumph when the Queen summoned George and his painting to Windsor Castle for the royal inspection.

George dined off his account of the interview for months, but the tangible results of the royal patronage were once again sadly overestimated. He even invited the young Prince of Wales to a private view (a notable convert that would have been), but there is no record of Edward ever having seen it. Meanwhile, the expenses of the exhibition were mounting alarmingly, and the provincial tour of the picture made a loss of two thousand pounds. Under all this financial pressure George finally buckled down to completing the engraving of 'The Worship of Bacchus', but the subscription committee had waited too long to recapture their initial enthusiasm.

The months lengthened into years, and now it seemed as if no one wanted to know about George's financial plight. The National Temperance League denied all responsibility for the provincial lecture tour, to which George wrote back furiously requiring to know, if they hadn't then 'who *had* sent the unfortunate picture upon its travels'.* He complained that he had raised a mortgage on his own property and lost the lot: he was 'hurt and indignant' that the League refused to cover any loss on a project that, after all, had been furthering their cause. He therefore cancelled his membership. To Sir Francis Crossley, who had been a leading light in the original committee of sponsors, he wrote asking for a loan of £500 at five per cent, signing himself pointedly 'Geo. Cruikshank who has lost a small fortune by endeavouring to save his fellow-creatures from destruction.'

By 1866 the situation was critical. In October another of the sponsors, John Taylor, put the situation bluntly to Cruikshank and offered a solution: 'I find that in a few days the loan upon the Cruikshank Gallery will again be due, and must be paid off or received at the heavy rate as heretofore. To pay off immediately we cannot manage, but the time when we must arrange to have it paid off as early as possible.'* His suggestion was that George's collection of etchings be sold which 'he was given to understand would realise a sum that would pay off all the advances made upon "The Worship of Bacchus"'. It was another ten years, in fact, before the collection was sold – to the Westminster Aquarium where it formed part of the permanent exhibition for some twenty-five years. But just in the bleakest hour George discovered he was not entirely forgotten: a testimonial subscription to help pay his debts was opened by, among others, John Ruskin (a devoted admirer of his early work). If the sum raised – nearly a thousand pounds – was less than expected, the roll-call of subscribers must surely have revived George's confidence: it read like a *Who's Who* of the art-world from Landseer to Whistler, of literature from Swinburne to Kingsley, of publishers, politicians and peers. Two years later, yet another committee assembled to purchase the painting itself for the nation and present it to the South Kensington Museum. George himself designed the subscription tickets – they showed the monster being dragged to its new home, like some huge block for the pyramids.

A monster it had become. If, as the teetotallers claimed, it made some converts hanging on the wall in South Kensington, no doubt George would have been well satisfied with his exertions. But as a work of art it was almost universally rejected. Frederick Stephens dismissed it as 'villainously executed as a whole and outrageously ridiculous in parts', and even his kindest critic, John Stewart, took pains to assure the public that the painting lacked finish because, strangely enough, it only formed the basis for the engraving, 'the more permanent' work. George embraced this theory with gratitude: years later he admitted to William Bates that the picture was 'never perfectly finished' and regretted that the regulations of the national gallery did not allow him to touch up the work after it had come into their possession! Today, it lies in the vaults of the Tate Gallery unseen, and virtually unseeable under the accumulations of grime and dust.

The fate of 'Bacchus' did not deter George from exhibiting – his 'Shakespeare on the stage of the Globe Theatre' was accepted for the Royal Academy in 1867 – still less from drumming up private commissions, which more than ever he now relied on. But for his pencil and etching-needle there were almost no takers: in 1875 he told one of the committee raised to purchase the Cruikshank collection at long last that he had not refused any offer of work lately, because there had been none – he 'had not made a shilling by his art for the last ten years'. That was more a figure of speech than a strict account of his cash-flow, but he must constantly have been oppressed by the feeling that the world now regarded him as a back number, and had closed the book on his career. George was still alive and active, but his life's achievements were now the province of the collectors, who wrote endlessly for choice specimens of the India proofs the artist had prudently hoarded, and of the cataloguers like George Reid (Keeper of Prints and Drawings at the British Museum) whose great *Descriptive Catalogue of George Cruikshank* was published in 1871.

For most of his admirers the artist personified a vanished era. To Ruskin, George was still the great interpreter of Grimm: in 1866, with sentimental memories of his own childhood, he privately commissioned some more sketches of nursery-land from

Cruikshank – only to find, when they arrived, that for him at least the spell was broken. For Richard Bentley (reconciled after twenty years with a hearty handshake in St James's Park one morning in 1864) George brought the old days back with a cheerfully grotesque frontispiece for his 1870 re-issue of *The Ingoldsby Legends*. But such titbits of work offered no solution to George's ever-present money problems: by nature he had always been one to offer charity rather than accept it, yet in his last years he could find no alternative – except outright poverty – to the benign efforts of well-wishers, subscription committees and testimonials. When, in 1867, he was awarded a pension of ninety-five pounds a year from the Civil List he hastened to assure the Prime Minister in his letter of thanks that 'this is a favour which I never should have thought of applying for myself, but some of my dear friends knowing my heavy pecuniary losses for many years past in working for the public good, without my knowledge made the application which has been so kindly responded to by your Lordship'.* At the same time he was also awarded a fifty-pound pension by the Royal Academy, from their Turner annuity funds. Even these modest tokens proved vulnerable to George's continuing lack of business acumen: when, six years later, yet another testimonial was being talked about, George wrote to *The Times* in answer to criticisms that he already received public and private pensions. He had, he explained, been induced to associate himself with a project to establish 'an Insurance Society for the Working Classes'. The scheme had proved fraudulent, and he personally had suffered a severe loss – as the fates had so often decreed in the past – from 'his efforts to save his fellow-creatures'. As for his pensions, he added, it would be a long time before they covered his losses.

George had developed into an indefatigable letter-writer to *The Times*. His contretemps with Ainsworth and his claims over *Oliver Twist* have been noted, but the preoccupations of his last ten years ranged over a most catholic spread of subjects from capital punishment to street accidents ('such a very important subject and I have had it in my mind for many years to prevent such a sacrifice of life'). Now he would be begging space from the Editor to advise his nephew Percy Cruikshank kindly not to designate himself 'George Cruikshank Jnr', so as to avoid confusion. Now he would be dilating on the aims and merits of the National Education League (of which he was a keen supporter and member of its deputation to Gladstone in the year of the Education Act).

He had been making public statements all his life, after all, in his prints and magazines, on platforms and in pamphlets. Even if his claims had sometimes been over-stated or his attitudes a shade inflexible, one had to admire his passionate concern for his fellow-creatures, which had not failed for sixty years to stir him to action.

During the debate surrounding the second Reform Bill in 1867, George abandoned his long political silence to inform the working-man of his best interests. He adapted and published an old design, calling it 'The British Bee-Hive' and purporting to show how the cell-like structure of society (with each 'worker' fulfilling his appointed role) had its microcosm in the highly efficient world of the bee-hive. Any attempt to tamper with this system, he declaimed in the long tract that accompanied the print, could only be to the detriment of the country as a whole. It had worked 'wonderfully well', indeed it was 'almost as perfect as it can be made by man'. The proposals for reform undermined the very basis of our government: 'If Universal Suffrage were granted, if everything were allowed, or even a great part of what is asked for, and *everyone* had a vote, it would cease to be a monarchy and would become a REPUBLIC.' Stay away from reform meetings, George advised, and distrust the agitators. 'From my experience in political matters for upwards of 50 years, I can declare that not one of the political agitators, when they happened to get into Parliament, ever did anything worth a straw.'

So the angry Radical of Peterloo had turned, in those mute years, into a high Tory (just as the hard-drinker of the *Tom and Jerry* period had been transfigured into the creator of 'Bacchus'), and George admitted as much in his text. But this change of view-point, to his way of thinking, involved no treachery to the working class. His sympathies were undiminished – after one of his regular 'visits to the poor' a friend found George weeping at what he had seen. It was just that unbridled voting, like unbridled drinking, would lead to social anarchy. His political views were now firmly welded to his temperance stand, and both were founded on a diagrammatic concept of society: the well-regulated activity of the 'Bee-Hive' was simply the desirable alternative to the chaos of 'The Worship of Bacchus'. Of course both sets of belief were suffused with the same, common Victorian fallacy, that if you get rid of the symptoms (drunkenness or political agitation) the causes will go away – but that is another discussion.

To the end of his days George was still seeking to create a monument in which the future might recognise his unfulfilled talents in the higher callings of Art, and still being doomed to disillusion and consequent disagreements. He might have believed 'The Worship of Bacchus' to have been that legacy, if his own generation could have shared that opinion. But it didn't. In May 1870 he thought he espied another opportunity coming his way, when he was invited by friends to join a committee devoted to the raising of a statue of Robert Bruce on the field of Bannockburn. It seemed so appropriate, as if destined – like him Bruce was a Scotsman who doggedly faced up to disappointment. 'Nil Desperandum' could have been his motto too.

George had no dreams of sculpting the proposed statue, but he did offer to design it and in no time, with the help of a sculptor friend, had produced a plaster model which was duly paraded before the Queen, the Press and the public. But then the snags arose: the public contributions were scanty, certainly nothing like enough to realise George's grand concept of a twelve-foot high bronze figure mounted on a twenty-two foot granite pedestal, and the whole scheme went into limbo. By the time it was revived the committee found that the proposed site on Bannockburn was now occupied by a flagpole, and Stirling Castle was agreed on as an alternative situation. This meant that the original pose (taken from George himself as the life-model) was quite inappropriate, and a completely new statue was needed. However, a row was already brewing between the artist and his colleagues over the question of expenses for the first model. 'Dr R. informed me that the committee were to pay £100, but more than double that sum would not compensate me for the large amount of time I have spent on this matter, and my friend Acton has not received anything for making the original model,' he wrote to the treasurer of the fund.* Clearly the committee were going to skimp, so he believed, on the whole venture, and sensing the drift George launched himself into an 'Address to the Scottish People', outlining the circumstances and adding, pointedly, what a great honour it would be to have his name as designer on the pedestal of the Bruce monument. Predictably, the committee now turned elsewhere for a design and when the modest stone effigy was finally unveiled in Stirling in November 1877 there was no Cruikshank by-line anywhere to be seen. Two months before his death George was firing off letters to *The Times* complaining of his treatment.

But George's real and enduring monument was the whole corpus of his published engravings, from that childhood sketch of Nelson's funeral-car in 1805 to his final plate (a frontispiece to Mrs Octavian Blewitt's *The Rose and the Lily*) in 1877: a unique record of nearly three generations, the prodigious harvest of a soaring imagination which at its highest was the work of truly 'inimitable' genius, and at its lowest never less than the work of a skilled craftsman. Whether George ever knew of it is not recorded, but, four years before he died, a concerted attempt to gain 'official' recognition of the artist's lifelong labours was made. A letter forwarded to Downing Street from the Duke of Argyll explains: 'The enclosed Memorial from the Grampian Club has been sent to the Duke of Argyll with a request that he would forward it to you. It recommends Mr George Cruikshank for the honour of knighthood and as the Duke is the President of the Club, he has consented to forward it. . . . He bids me to add however that he would like you to explain to Mr Gladstone that he makes no application but simply sends the Memorial on.' The memorial read:

> For upwards of 50 years Mr Cruikshank has enjoyed the highest celebrity as
> an artist while his artistic powers have uniformly been put forth in support
> of sound morals and good government. For a considerable period Mr
> Cruikshank served as Lt-Colonel of a regiment of volunteers raised by his
> patriotism, and latterly he has devoted the principal share of his time to
> works of philanthropy.*

In true Civil Service fashion a memorandum, in an anonymous hand, is attached to the memorial. It curtly outlines the hard realities of departmental protocol: 'I think there can be no doubt that there is not a case. The Memorial mentions 1. his merits as an artist, 2. his services as Lt-Col. of volunteers. In both lines there are very many others far superior to him. There is actually no artist so rewarded since Sir E. Landseer's death. Sir F. Grant, Sir W. Boxall and Sir J. Gilbert being knighted in virtue of their offices.'

So it was as plain George that he celebrated his Silver Wedding on 8 March 1875, attended by a guard of honour from his old corps. Walter Hamilton, knowing the secret of Augustus Street, thought the whole thing a mockery and was moved by Eliza's obvious concern when George was overwrought by the excitement of the occasion. But to most of the guests it was the same old George, ever ready with a joke, always threatening to break into a hornpipe or a verse of 'Lord Bateman': it was as if (remarked a friend, quoting Dickens) he had grown old, got over it and grown young again. Even three weeks before his death, another recalled, he was the same 'bright brave-spirited old man' who could be seen 'hurrying along the streets with cheerful, eager aspect to keep "a business appointment"'.

'Reverently attentive . . . have I and Watts Phillips', recalled Sala, 'sat smoking our pipes (long churchwarden pipes, I am ashamed to say, Madam) and listened to the brave old man telling how plates were best polished, or oil- or whiting-rubbed, or roughened with emery powder; how the burnisher, the scraper, the dry-point and even the glazier's diamond should be used on copper, and how to conduct the crucial process of hammering-up a portion of a plate which had been too deeply bitten in.' Sala and Watts Phillips (whom George outlived by four years) were his pupils, but Cruikshank left behind him no School or disciples. The secrets of his craft he willingly passed on, but his art was in the truest sense 'inimitable'. It was the product of the man and of his times, and it was the tragedy of George's career that when those times passed, his art (so far as the public was concerned) became obsolete.

In a way, George may be said never to have really grown up. His vision of the world was essentially childlike in its simplicity and candour. Said *Punch* in one of the most perceptive of many obituaries:

> His nature had something childlike in its transparency. You saw through him completely. There was neither wish nor effort to disguise his self-complacency, his high appreciation of himself, his delight in the appreciation of others, any more than there was to make himself out better, or cleverer, or more unselfish than his neighbours. In him England has lost one who was, in every sense, as true a man as he was a rare and original genius, and a pioneer in the arts of illustration.

Maybe that was why George's work reminded so many – like Ruskin and Thackeray – of their own childhoods. Even in maturity George's behaviour in public frequently struck his friends as childish – appealing and lovable but certainly not carrying the dignity of his years. And even in private (as for instance in his letters to friends) he would lapse into the idioms and expressions of childhood. Yet it was one of his greatest virtues, too, that he continued to observe the world with the freshness and wonderment of a child. It was what enabled him to isolate all that was odd or funny or ridiculous, even frightening, around him. His excursions into fantasy and fairyland were a glorious extension of this: his imagination was not constrained by those adult inhibitions that shut the door on this magic world. Equally, it also accounted for the relative failure of his more ambitious projects – when it tried to embrace the whole world (as in 'Passing Events' or 'The Worship of Bacchus') it declined into fussiness and over-elaboration.

But to reduce the world thus to miniature was perhaps an attempt to try to cope with it, to make it comprehensible. So much of George's life was occupied with the effort of coping – coping with money, with business relationships, with drink, with friends (whose loyalty moved him deeply and whose defection desolated him). So it is no surprise that when George turned his hand to his autobiographical or 'posterity' plates he could not – or did not – get beyond his adolescence. And in later life he resisted the onset of old age with all his might, trying to match the fitness of younger men even as he endeavoured to cover up his bald patch by coaxing his hair into place with an elastic band.

In the middle of January 1878 George developed bronchitis, took to his bed, and for the first time in his life failed to get 'at it again'. He died on 1 February at the age of eighty-six, refusing a 'medicinal' glass of brandy to his last breath, and was temporarily buried at Kensal Green. His funeral would have taken place – as the Movement intended for one of its doughtiest warriors – in the crypt of St Paul's Cathedral, but that was closed for repairs. Only the following November could the marble inscription ('George Cruikshank, Artist, Designer, Etcher, Painter. In memory of his Genius and his Art, his matchless Industry and worthy Work for all his fellow men') be placed in position. In the afternoon of the 29th a modest little procession climbed Ludgate Hill to his last resting-place, a hearse, a mourning-coach, and four sergeants of the Volunteers. No bands, no banners, and probably no little boy sitting sketching on the kerbside.

Appendix

Letters from George Cruikshank to Harrison Ainsworth concerning the text of *The Tower of London*.

This one, dated 16 September 1840, shows that George had visualised the episode of the attack on the Byward Tower in great detail before Ainsworth wrote the text. George's description in the letter is followed almost exactly in the book.

> The Party under the command of Sir Thos Wyat were divided into *two divisions* – one of which proceeded along 'Thames Street' – the other by 'Tower St.' – the 'Bulwark Gate' was soon carried & the wooden houses adjoining in flames – 'in no time' a terrible struggle takes place at the 'Lions Gate' Sir Thomas succeeds in forcing this gate also – and drives all before him – and before the Portcullis of the 'Middle Tower' can be lowered it is propped up by a piece of timber, Wyat dashes across the Bridge amongst the vanquished who are flying to the 'Bye Ward Tower' from which issue the three Giants – in Helmets & Curass Og & Magog (armed with maces – Gog has a Partizan – Og knocks about in fine style & bundles a lot of fellows over the wall Magog (who has a shield) has enough to do to keep back Wyat, who tries to gallop over him, one well aimed & desperate blow from Sir Thomas – would have brought down the Giant had he not caught it on his shield – at the same instant an awful crack from Magog's mace splits the skull of the Noble Animal upon which Sir Thomas was mounted – the fall of their leader daunted the attacking party – the moments delay gave the treating party time to pass into the gateway of the Byward & Lower the Portcullis – during this affair Xit had mounted on the wall – in a most noble manner – & whilst flourishing his sword and daring them to come on he perceives someone who had been thrown into the Ditch endeavouring to climb the wall – he calls out to him to surrender – which he does This may be a person of consequence . . . .
> NB there are two more Horsemen besides Sir Thos upon the Bridge – (in armour of course).
> PS. Sir Thos's party had taken possession of the Middle Tower – from which they fired upon those who were firing from the Byward so now I leave you in the 'thick of it' – the post of honour! so fire away! my boy – fight on! and success attend you

This next letter adds further details, which were also incorporated into the text.

> I enclose the tracing for the 'Guy' [*Guy Fawkes*, the novel they were both working on concurrently] – which has cost me some trouble, as I made two drawings and was much puzzled which to choose – however this one *must* do. As it is highly improbable that little 'Xit' would be in armour I send you a sketch of the manner in which I have dressed him up. His Helmet being much too large for him and surmounted with a very fine plume of feathers – I am in a dreadful state of anxiety about my plates. There is such a *frightful* quantity of work in them – Hoping you are getting on well – and that you are well.

Sketched on the letter are two drawings of Xit, as described. The following letter deals with an important scene a little later on – the illustration for which was indeed called 'The Death Warrant' as Cruikshank suggests.

> Had we not better change the title to 'The Death Warrant'? Mind there is no dagger. Simon grasps his sword with his *left* hand. The Right arm is merely extended & the hand clenched – I have received an answer from the Chamberlain with consents, and a note from Mr Swift who presents his compliments to you and is quite ready now to show us the 'Lions' in his Tower. Shall I write to say we will be with him on the second of next month?

And this final letter deals with the important episode of Lady Jane Grey's execution.

> These few lines in case I should not see you – the first sketch of Jane meeting the body of her husband is thus. . . . Now as the bearers would certainly not (nor could they) carry the body up the stairs – they must of course take it up the road – and as they would do this without being seen until they came up close to the scaffold the other appears more natural – and will group better thus.

Plates

3

Publish'd Apr. 6, 1807, by LAURIE & WHITTLE, 53 Fleet Street, London.

Cruickshank Del.

COUNTRY LIFE,

CONTRASTED WITH THE PLEASURES OF TOWN;

Written by CAPTAIN MORRIS; *with additional Stanzas by the late Mr.* HEWERDINE, *marked by inverted Commas.*

3 COUNTRY LIFE
Isaac and George Cruikshank
(1807). This illustration to one of
Laurie and Whittle's songsheets is
generally attributed as one of
George's earliest collaborations
with his father.

4 A REPUBLICAN BELLE
Isaac Cruikshank (1794). A
characteristically anti-Gallic
broadside by the elder Cruikshank,
published during the first coalition
against France.

Pub. March 10 1794 by S. W. Fores N° 3 Piccadilly who has fitted up his Caricature Exhibition in an Entire novel stile admit 1.

= N.B. folios lent out.

A REPUBLICAN BELLE.
A Picture of PARIS for 1794.

5

6

5 THE ROYAL EXTINGUISHER
Isaac Cruikshank (1795). One of
Isaac's Pittite productions,
celebrating his Treasonable
Practices Bill. Pitt, as a watchman,
extinguishes a seditious meeting of
Fox, Sheridan and their followers
at Copenhagen House.

6 PRINCELY AMUSEMENTS
George Cruikshank. Satire on the
Royal Family from *The Scourge*
(1812) For full description, see
page 15.

The CORONATION of the EMPRESS of the NAIRS.

Boney Hatching a Bulletin or Snug Winter Quarters!!!

7 THE CORONATION OF THE
EMPRESS OF THE NAIRS
George Cruikshank. From *The
Scourge* (1812). For further details,
see page 15.

8 BONEY HATCHING A BULLETIN
George Cruikshank (1812).
Published during Napoleon's
retreat from Moscow as later
bulletins began to reveal the extent
of the disaster.

BROKEN GINGERBREAD

9 BROKEN GINGERBREAD
George Cruikshank (1814). Sequel to Gillray's satire on Napoleon baking his gingerbread kings (1806). Here the fallen Emperor is ludicrously hawking his wares for export from Elba.

10 THE MARRIAGE TO JOSEPHINE
George Cruikshank (1815). Plate from Dr Syntax's 'hudibrastic poem' *The Life of Napoleon*.

11 THE FLIGHT FROM EGYPT
George Cruikshank (1812). Further plate from *The Life of Napoleon*, ridiculing the Emperor's 'desertion' of his beleaguered army in Egypt 1799.

12 A SWARM OF ENGLISH BEES
George Cruikshank (1816). A satire on the post-war passion for Napoleonic mementoes.

A Swarm of English Bees hiving in the Imperial Carriage!!   Who would have thought it   !!! !!! !!!

A Scene at the LONDON museum Piccadilly, or A peep at the Spoils of Ambition, taken at the Battle of Waterloo being a new Tax on John Bull for 1816 &c &c—

Pub'd by H Humphrey St James's St London June 1816

13 THE BLESSINGS OF PEACE
George Cruikshank (1816).
George's outburst against the
restrictive corn laws – see page 23.

14 A FREE BORN ENGLISHMAN
George Cruikshank (1819). Wry
comment, adapted from an earlier
design, on the passing of the Six
Acts. See page 33.

A FREE BORN ENGLISHMAN!
THE ADMIRATION of the WORLD!!!
AND THE ENVY of SURROUNDING NATIONS!!!!!

15 POOR BULL AND HIS BURDEN
George Cruikshank (1819). A
Radical's view of the tyranny of
wealth and privilege.

Massacre at St Peters or "BRITONS STRIKE HOME"!!!

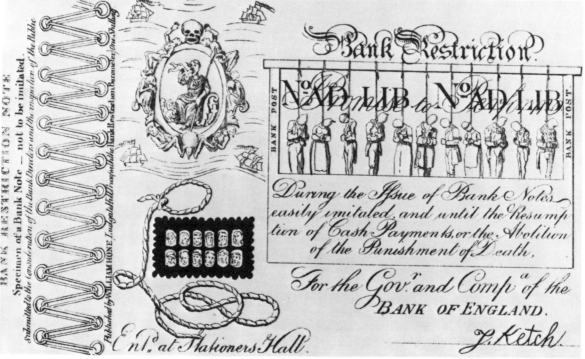

16 BRITONS STRIKE HOME!
George Cruikshank (1819). Satire
published within a week of the
Peterloo massacre. See page 30.

17 BANK NOTE – NOT TO BE
IMITATED
George Cruikshank (1819).
George's 'counterfeit' bank
restriction note – his protest

against the death penalty for
forging and passing bank notes,
and which he (later) claimed was
instrumental in getting the law
itself changed.

18

Give not thy strength unto women, nor thy ways to that which destroyeth kings.

Solomon.

18 QUALIFICATION
George Cruikshank (1820).
Woodcut from Hone's pamphlet
The Queen's Matrimonial Ladder.
The Prince Regent in an
advanced stage of dissipation.

19 Woodcut from Hone's THE
POLITICAL SHOWMAN AT HOME
George Cruikshank (1821), being a
copy of the artist's illuminated
transparency hung outside Hone's
shop to celebrate Queen Caroline's
triumph. Freedom, Caroline and
the Printing Press here together
banish their political enemies to
outer darkness.

20 (Autobiographical)
Woodcut from Hone's *Facetiae and
Miscellanies* (1828). Hone (left) and
George in friendly consultation.

21 THE PICCADILLY NUISANCE
George Cruikshank (1818).
Congestion and chaos in the streets
of Regency London.

22 INCONVENIENCES OF A
CROWDED DRAWING-ROOM
George Cruikshank (1818). High
society at home – see page 42.

MONSTROSITIES of 1819. & 1820.

I do not see why Ladies should not have a Lark as well as the Gentlemen

23 MONSTROSITIES OF 1819/20
George Cruikshank (1819).
Dandified fashions on parade: one
of the series of 'monstrosities'
which appeared from 1816 to 1828.

24 THE LADIES' ACCELERATOR
Robert Cruikshank (1819). Satire
on the latest craze in locomotion,
the cumbersome and short-lived
velocipede.

25

26

25 MR B. MASTHEADED
George Cruikshank (1820). Fourth
plate in *The Midshipman's Progress*,
from a design by Frederick
Marryat.

26 THE COMFORTS OF A
CABRIOLET
George Cruikshank (1821). Swells
in a spot of difficulty with their
new-fangled 'cabs'.

A Party of Pleasure.————— Dedicated to the Funny Club—

Monstrosities of 1822—

27 A PARTY OF PLEASURE
George Cruikshank (1822). From a
design by Frederick Marryat.

28 MONSTROSITIES OF 1822
George Cruikshank (1822). A
further instalment of George's
sartorial satires.

29

30

29 LIFE IN LONDON
George and Robert Cruikshank
(1820). Tom and Jerry at the
Olympic Coffee House, after a
night slumming it with 'low life' in
London.

30 LIFE IN LONDON
George and Robert Cruikshank
(1820). Tom and Jerry in the Salon
at Covent Garden, observing the
parade of the Cyprians (high-class
ladies of easy virtue).

31 LIFE IN LONDON
George and Robert Cruikshank
(1820). Tom and Jerry getting the
better of a Charley. Charleys or
public watchmen, the predecessors
of the police, suffered a severe bout
of baiting after the publication of
Life in London.

32 THE BLUE DEVILS!
George Cruikshank (1823).
George's impish study in
depression.

33/34 GRIMMS' FAIRY TALES
George Cruikshank (1823).
Woodcut vignettes from the first
English edition of the *Fairy Tales*.

35 POINTS OF HUMOUR
George Cruikshank (1823).
Illustration to Burns's poem of
The Jolly Beggars.

36 POINTS OF HUMOUR
George Cruikshank (1823). The
Cardinal's Fall.

37 OLD BUMBLEHEAD THE XVIII
TRYING ON NAPOLEON'S BOOTS
George Cruikshank (1823). Satire on the French king's invasion of
Spain, to aid Ferdinand VII against
his rebels.

38 NASHIONAL TASTE!!
George Cruikshank (1824). John
Nash spiked on the spire of one of
his own churches (All Souls,
Langham Place). See page 41.

The POLITICAL.TOY-MAN.

39 THE POLITICAL TOYMAN
Robert Cruikshank (1825).
Robert's parody on Lord
Brougham and his pioneering
projects for the education of the
working class.

40

Beauties of BRIGHTON

40 BEAUTIES OF BRIGHTON
George Cruikshank (1826). The
fashionable parade in front of
George IV's Royal Pavilion. From
a design by Alfred Crowquill
(pictured here as one of the trio of
swells, left).

41 PHILOPROGENITIVENESS
George Cruikshank (1826). Plate
from *Phrenological Illustrations*,
satires on Dr Gall's system of
phrenology. See page 53.

41

Philoprogenitiveness

42 ILLUSTRATIONS OF TIME
George Cruikshank (1827).
Frontispiece from the artist's
second venture as his own
publisher.

43 IGNORANCE IS BLISS
George Cruikshank (1828). Comic
vignette from the first book of
Scraps and Sketches.

44

LONDON going out of Town — or — The March of Bricks & Mortar.

45

44 LONDON GOING OUT OF TOWN
George Cruikshank (1829). On the erosion of the countryside by London's expanding suburbs. From *Scraps and Sketches*. See page 56.

45 THE GIN SHOP
George Cruikshank (1829). From the second book of *Scraps and Sketches*, a comment on the exploitation of the new gin-palaces. See page 57.

46 THE·FIEND'S FRYING PAN
George Cruikshank (1832).
George's satire, in *Scraps and
Sketches*, on the debauchery
prevalent at the annual St
Bartholomew's Fair in Smithfield.

47 THE KNACKER'S YARD
George Cruikshank (1831).
Illustration to the animal welfare
pamphlet *The Voice of Humanity*.

48 SALUS POPULI SUPREMA LEX
George Cruikshank (1832). Attack
on the Southwark Water Works
company, inspired by a serious
outbreak of cholera in the capital.
See page 60.

49 SWEEPING MEASURES
George Cruikshank (1832). One of
the artist's two Reform satires,
showing Lord John Russell
brushing a cloud of verminous
borough-mongers out of the
Commons.

*From the Drawing by Maclise
originally published in
Fraser's Magazine.*

50 Portrait of George Cruikshank
by Daniel Maclise, from *Fraser's
Magazine* (1833).

51 George Cruikshank tweaking
the nose of the errant publisher,
Kidd. From the *Sketchbook* (1834).

52 THE GIN JUGGERNAUTH
George Cruikshank (1835). Pre-
Temperance era attack on the evils
of drink. From the *Sketchbook*.

The GIN JUGGARNATH. or, The Worship of the GREAT SPIRIT of the age.
It's Devotees destroy themselves — It's progress is marked with desolation, misery and crime.

Pit. Boxes & Gallery.

MARCH.

53 PIT, BOXES AND GALLERY
George Cruikshank (1836). Study
of three levels of London society
from the final issue of the
Sketchbook.

54 MARCH
George Cruikshank. Illustration to
the 1835 *Comic Almanack*. A windy
day outside the shop of George's
publisher in Fleet Street. Just
inside the door Cruikshank himself
can be seen in conversation with
Charles Tilt.

55

JUNE.

56

AUGUST.——Bathing at Brighton

AUGUST. Regatta.

59 VAUXHALL GARDENS
George Cruikshank (1836/7). Plate
from *Sketches by Boz*.

PUBLIC DINNERS
George Cruikshank (1836/7). From
Sketches by Boz. Dickens (centre)
and Cruikshank (right) themselves
have been introduced into the
picture.

61 FAGIN IN THE CONDEMNED
CELL
George Cruikshank (1837/8).
Plate to *Oliver Twist*. For
background to this illustration see
page 69.

62

62 THE LAST CHANCE
George Cruikshank (1837/8). Bill
Sykes's final scene in *Oliver Twist*.

63

63 Pencil Sketch, and suggested
captions from George to Dickens,
for plate to *Oliver Twist* (1837/8).

64 THE WITCHES' FROLIC
George Cruikshank (1838).
Illustration to Barham's *Ingoldsby
Legends* published in *Bentley's
Miscellany*.

64

65 JACK SHEPPARD CARVING HIS
NAME ON THE BEAM
George Cruikshank (1839). Plate to
Ainsworth's *Jack Sheppard*.

66

george Cruikshank

66 THE WELL HOLE
George Cruikshank (1839).
Jonathan Wild throwing Sir
Rowland Trenchard down the well
hole, a scene from *Jack Sheppard*.

67 THE LAST SONG
George Cruikshank (1838).
Grimaldi, the great clown, making
his farewell performance. From
Memoirs of Grimaldi, edited by
Dickens.

Designed Etched & Published by George Cruikshank. 1839

Lord Bateman as he appeared previous to his embarkation.

68 THE LOVING BALLAD OF LORD
BATEMAN
George Cruikshank (1839). Lord
Bateman previous to his
embarkation for foreign parts –
first plate from Cruikshank's
illustrations to his famous song.

Designed Etched & Published by George Cruikshank 1839

The Proud young Porter, in Lord Bateman's State Apartment —

69 THE LOVING BALLAD OF LORD
BATEMAN
George Cruikshank (1839). The
Proud Young Porter, a later
episode in the adventures of Lord
Bateman.

70 Portrait of George Cruikshank
from *The Omnibus* (1841)
accompanied by his distinctive
signature.

71 MASQUE IN THE PALACE
GARDENS
George Cruikshank (1839). Plate
from Ainsworth's *Tower of London*.

72 George's cartoon of his
supposedly frightening appearance
in public – see page 61. From
The Omnibus (1841).

73 GHOSTS
George Cruikshank (1841).
Illustration to article on the
supernatural in *The Omnibus*.

74/75 Preliminary sketches to
Dibden's Songs Naval and National:
George Cruikshank (1841).

George Cruikshank

76 SIR BULKELEY PRICE
BRINGING THE MORTGAGE
MONEY
George Cruikshank (1842).
Illustration to Ainsworth's *The
Miser's Daughter*.

77 HENRY VIII AND ANNE
BOLEYN
George Cruikshank (1843).
Illustration to Ainsworth's *Windsor
Castle*.

George Cruikshank

Mʳ Lambkin, finding that he has been variously and thoroughly be-
-fooled, foolishly dashes into dissipation to drown his distressful
thoughts – He joins Jovial society and sings "The right end of Life
is to live and be jolly !"

78 THE BACHELOR'S OWN BOOK
George Cruikshank (1844).

George Cruikshank

Mr. Lambkin being quite recovered, with the aid of new milk and Sea Breezes, determines to reform his habits, but feels buried alive in the Grand Mausoleum Club; and, contemplating an old bachelor member who sits poring over the newspapers all day, he feels horrorstruck at the probability of such a fate becoming his own, and determines to seek a reconciliation with the Lady of his Affections.

79 Episodes in the adventures of
Mr Lambkin (Gent) 'in pursuit of
pleasure and amusement'.

80

80 THE TRIUMPH OF CUPID
George Cruikshank (1845). George
(and spaniel) in his fireside reverie.
Plate from *The Table-Book*. See page
83.

The Folly of Crime.

81 THE FOLLY OF CRIME
George Cruikshank (1845).
Allegorical plate from *The Table-Book*. See page 83.

The Height of Improvement – putting up the Shutters

OVER POPULATION

82 THE HEIGHT OF
IMPROVEMENT
George Cruikshank. Skit on the
mushrooming new department
stores, with their shop-windows
several storeys high. From the
1843 *Comic Almanack.*

83 OVERPOPULATION
George Cruikshank. George's
answer to overcrowding in
London, from the 1851 *Comic
Almanack.*

84 BORN A GENIUS AND BORN A
DWARF
George Cruikshank. Bitter
comment on the tragedy of the
painter Haydon and success of Tom
Thumb (right) – see page 81. From
the 1847 *Comic Almanack.*

85–88 Plates 3, 5, 6 and 8 from
The Bottle
George Cruikshank (1847). The
decline and fall of a family whose
parents take to drink.

BORN A GENIUS AND BORN A DWARF.

PLATE III.——AN EXECUTION SWEEPS OFF THE GREATER PART OF THEIR FURNITURE: THEY COMFORT THEMSELVES WITH THE BOTTLE.

86

Plate V. —— COLD, MISERY, AND WANT, DESTROY THEIR YOUNGEST CHILD: THEY CONSOLE THEMSELVES WITH THE BOTTLE.

87

Plate VI. —— FEARFUL QUARRELS, AND BRUTAL VIOLENCE, ARE THE NATURAL CONSEQUENCES OF THE FREQUENT USE OF THE BOTTLE.

PLATE VIII ——— THE BOTTLE HAS DONE ITS WORK — IT HAS DESTROYED THE INFANT AND THE MOTHER, IT HAS BROUGHT THE SON AND THE DAUGHTER TO VICE AND TO THE STREETS, AND HAS LEFT THE FATHER A HOPELESS MANIAC.

89 THE DRUNKARD'S CHILDREN
George Cruikshank (1848). Plate 2
of the sequel to *The Bottle*.

90 THE CAT DID IT!
George Cruikshank (1847).
Illustration to Mayhew's
The Greatest Plague of Life.

90

91

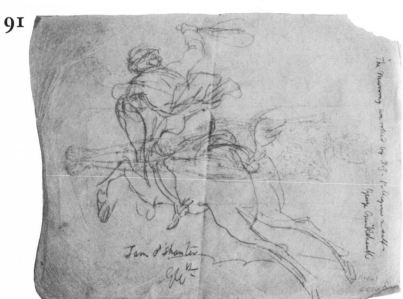

91 Pencil Sketch for Cruikshank's
painting *Tam O'Shanter*,
superimposed on an earlier sketch
for an illustration to Pettigrew's
History of Egyptian Mummies (publ.
1834).

92 HOP-O'-MY-THUMB
George Cruikshank (1853).
Frontispiece to the first book of
The Fairy Library.

Hop'o'my Thumb & the Seven League Boots

The Father proposes to lose the Children !!!

They Leave Hop'o'my Thumb and his Brothers in the Wood

George Cruikshank

93

The Fairies tie the Giant up in the Bean-Stalk

94

95

Passing Events, or The Tail of the Comet of 1853

93 JACK AND THE BEANSTALK
George Cruikshank (1854).
Illustration to the second book of
The Fairy Library.

94 THE FOUR MIGHTY SERVANTS
George Cruikshank (1854). Plate
from the English edition of *The
Pentamerone*, Basile's Italian stories.

95 PASSING EVENTS
George Cruikshank (1854). Epic
frontispiece to the first issue of
George Cruikshank's Magazine.

96 DESIGN FOR A PAINTING
George Cruikshank (n.d.) A typical
Cruikshankian sketch, with figures
pencilled in in any available corner.

97 THE RUNAWAY KNOCK
George Cruikshank (1855). Oil
painting.

97

The Rose and the Lily

98 FALSTAFF'S GRAND
MANOEUVRE
George Cruikshank (1857). Plate
from Brough's *Life of Sir John
Falstaff.*

99 AN UNEXPECTED REBUKE
George Cruikshank (1857). Plate
from Brough's *Life of Sir John
Falstaff.*

100 THE ROSE AND THE LILY
George Cruikshank (1877).
Frontispiece to Mrs Octavian
Blewitt's book – George's last
published illustration.

101   Engraved portrait of George Cruikshank *c.* 1870.

Notes

CHAPTER 1. 'CRADLED IN CARICATURE'

2   *Andrew Crookshanks.* E. B. Krumbhaar, *Isaac Cruikshank*, introduction.

5   *until 1895.* Drawings by George Cruikshank, ed. Sir B. W. Richardson. The same drawings, with additions and notes by Charles Hancock, were reissued in 1896 as *A Handbook for Posterity or Recollections of Twiddle Twaddle.*

6   *of all degrees.* Frederic Stephens, *A Memoir of George Cruikshank*, p. 7.

6   *as a 'boy'.* C. C. Kohler, 'Catalogue of George Cruikshank Sale', ref. 262–9.

7   *press-gang incident.* H. S. Ashbee, in *Notes and Queries*, 5th series, vol. 9, 9 Feb 1878, p. 119.

7   *as he recounts.* George Cruikshank, *A Pop-Gun Fired Off in Defence of the British Volunteers of 1803.*

8   *some of his copper plates.* Cruikshank to G. W. Reid, 1870, quoted in Reid's *Descriptive Catalogue of the Works of George Cruikshank.*

8   *over the bookshop.* G. S. Layard, *George Cruikshank's Portraits of Himself.*

9   *told his cataloguer.* Cruikshank to G. W. Reid, 1870, quoted in Reid's *Catalogue.*

9   *but an actor. . . .'* Kohler, 'Catalogue', ref. 53.

10   *conversations with George).* Handbook for *Posterity*, plate 15.

11   *yearnings after stardom.* Only on authority of William Bates, *George Cruikshank, the Artist, the Humorist and the Man*, pp. 9–10.

11   *with general approval.* Alice Thompson, in *The Magazine of Art*, March 1880.

CHAPTER 2. PERSONALITIES

13   *sympathising roar.* W. M. Thackeray, 'Essay on the Genius of George Cruikshank', *Westminster Review*, Aug 1840.

16   *the offensive paragraph.* The Scourge, March 1812.

16   *the original plate.* G. S. Layard, *Suppressed Plates.*

17   *the Agitator.* George Cruikshank's *Omnibus* (1841), no. 1, p. 28.

19   *prosecuted in November.* The Examiner, Nov 1815.

20   *only to 'drilling'.* Undated draft, Cruikshank Collection, Middlesex Records Office.

21   *of the regulars.* George Cruikshank, *A Pop-Gun Fired Off in Defence of the British Volunteers of 1803.*

CHAPTER 3. RADICALS AND ROYALISTS

24   *honourable disposition.'* Hone to Mrs

Cruikshank, quoted in Fred Hackwood, *William Hone, His Life and Times*, p. 190.

24 *in the evenings.'* Ibid.

25 *strictest morality.'* C.C.Kohler, 'Catalogue of George Cruikshank Sale', ref. 56.

25 *that same hospital. George Cruikshank's Omnibus* (1841), no. 1, p. 3.

26 *respectable people.'* Jas. H.F., 'George Cruikshank', *Biographical Magazine*, vol. 3 (1852), p. 108.

28 *hand them the change.* Cruikshank to Whitaker, 1875, quoted in Blanchard Jerrold, *The Life of George Cruikshank*, 2nd ed., p. 59.

34 *treated her so foully.* W.M.Thackeray, 'Essay on the Genius of George Cruikshank', *Westminster Review*, Aug 1840.

35 *ideas and feelings.'* William Hone, *Aspersions Answered* (1824), p. 49.

36 *immoral situation.'* Dorothy M. George, *British Museum Catalogue of Political and Personal Satires*, vol. x, p. xl.

37 *mind and household.'* Hone to Cruikshank, quoted in A.M.Cohn, *Catalogue Raisonné of the Works of George Cruikshank*, introduction.

37 *bowls of punch!* Hackwood, *Hone*, p. 249.

CHAPTER 4. LIFE IN LONDON

41 *working out its objects. George Cruikshank's Omnibus* (1841), no. 1, p. 2.

43 *available opportunity.* Henry Vizetelly, *Glances Back through Seventy Years*, p. 106.

43 *to suck eggs!'* Hone to Cruikshank, quoted in A.M.Cohn, *Catalogue Raisonné of the Works of George Cruikshank*, introduction.

43 *up-and-down tussle.'* G.A.Sala, in *Gentleman's Magazine*, May 1878.

43 *pet of the Fancy.'* Ibid.

44 *had not contemplated.'* William Bates, *George Cruikshank, the Artist, the Humorist and the Man*, p. 23.

46 *tip of his tongue.'* Blanchard Jerrold, *The Life of George Cruikshank*, 2nd ed., p. 82.

47 *beef-steak and bowl. . . .* 'Lectures on the Fine Arts', *Blackwood's Edinburgh Magazine*, July 1823.

47 *has suggested.* David Borowitz, 'George Cruikshank – Mirror of an Age', paper to William Andrews Clark Library Seminar, 1970.

48 *'stout lady'.* Dickens to Ainsworth, Jan 1838, *Letters of Charles Dickens*, ed. Madeleine House and Graham Storey, vol. 1, p. 358.

49 *queer places.'* Jerrold, *Cruikshank*, 2nd ed., p. 109.

49 *almost disconcerting. Fraser's Magazine*, Aug 1833.

49 *before the public.* Cruikshank to William Bates, 30 April 1873.

51 *gems of humour.'* *Somerset House Gazette*, 1824.

52 *Oberon and Titania.'* W.M.Thackeray, 'Essay on the Genius of George Cruikshank', *Westminster Review*, Aug 1840.

54 *generous and tender.* Ibid.

55 *the stone again.'* cf. note by Cruikshank, Middlesex Records Office (534/14a).

55 *blotting paper.* Cruikshank to James Robins, 24 Aug 1825, quoted in F. Marchmont, *The Three Cruikshanks.*

55 *according to the publisher.* William Hone, *Aspersions Answered* (1824), p. 18.

CHAPTER 5. THE FACTS OF FICTION

60 *in due subjection.'* Dickens to Ainsworth, Jan 1838 (MS., comtesse de Suzannet).

60 *According to his son. Notes and Queries,* 5th series, vol. 9, 15 June 1878.

61 *to Ainsworth.* Blanchard Jerrold to Ainsworth, *c.*1840, quoted in S. M. Ellis, *Ainsworth and His Friends.*

61 *of seeming rude.* James Grant, *Portraits of Public Characters,* 2 vols (1841).

62 *on my entrance.'* George Cruikshank's *Omnibus* (1841), no. 1, p. 5.

62 *metropolitan police.'* Dickens to Felton, July 1842, quoted in John Forster's *Life of Dickens,* 3 vols (1872–4).

64 *highly as myself.'* Dickens to Macrone, Nov 1835 (MS., Huntington Library).

65 *not work at all.'* Cruikshank to Macrone, Oct 1836, quoted in A. de Suzannet, *Catalogue d'un choix de livres imprimés* (1925).

65 *back to Macrone.* Dickens to Macrone, Oct 1836 (MS., Morgan Library).

66 *if convenient.'* Dickens to Cruikshank, Nov 1837 (MS., Gimbel Collection, Yale University).

67 *book of forfeits.'* Forster to Bentley, Nov 1838 (MS., Berg Collection).

67 *lots of stippling.* G. S. Layard, *Suppressed Plates.*

67 *characters are mine.'* cf. R. A. Vogler, 'A Reassessment of the Role of Artist and Author', *Princeton University Library Chronicle,* vol. XXXV (1973–4).

68 *has pointed out.* John Harvey, *Victorian Novelists and Their Illustrators.*

70 *heard of him.* Cruikshank to Mackenzie, Jan 1872 (MS., Historical Society of Pennsylvania).

70 *lists of notes.* For a more detailed description of the sheet, see Vogler, 'Reassessment'.

72 *to be philosophical.* Dickens to Felton, March 1843 (MS., Berg Collection).

72 *illustrious George!'* Dickens to Ainsworth, Dec 1838, in *The Letters of Charles Dickens,* ed. Madeleine House and Graham Storey, vol. 1.

72 *agreeable, to the last.'* Cruikshank to Dickens, Feb 1841 (MS., Huntington Library).

73 *a good fellow!'* Ainsworth to Macrone, March 1836, quoted in Ellis, *Ainsworth and His Friends.*

73 *comedy and manners.'* Ainsworth to Macrone, Nov 1836, in ibid.

73 *than the writer's.'* W. M. Thackeray, 'Essay on the Genius of George Cruikshank', *Westminster Review,* Aug 1840.

74 *the present Regent Street.'* G. A. Sala, in *Gentleman's Magazine,* vol. CCXLII, 1878.

74 *really quit of him.* Cruikshank to Ainsworth, March 1840, quoted in Ellis, *Ainsworth and His Friends.*

75 *portion of the work.* Ainsworth, June 1840, in ibid.

77 *mild letter to The Times.* Cruikshank to Editor of *The Times,* 8 April 1872.

CHAPTER 6. MORALS FOR THE MILLIONS

81 *Ainsworth in March.* Cruikshank to Ainsworth, March 1841, quoted in S. M. Ellis, *Ainsworth and His Friends.*

82 *honour or integrity.* Cruikshank to Ainsworth, in ibid.

83 *had called it.* Dickens to Cruikshank, May 1841 (MS., Gimbel Collection, Yale University).

83 *to do good.'* George Cruikshank draft, Middlesex Records Office (534/14a).

84 *big, big!'* G. S. Layard, *George Cruikshank's Portraits of Himself.*

84 *most searching glances.* Henry Vizetelly, *Glances Back through Seventy Years,* p. 106.

85 *tired of the thing. . . .'* Thackeray to Carmichael-Smyth, Dec 1839, in *Letters and Private Papers of W. M. Thackeray,* ed. Gordon N. Ray, vol. 1, p. 395.

85 *author wrote to him.* Thackeray to Cruikshank, May 1839, in ibid. vol. 1, p. 380

87 *works of art.'* Cruikshank draft letter to Editor of *Aesthetic Review* (n.d.), Middlesex Records Office (534/14a).

87 *George, I suppose.* Dickens to Forster, quoted in Blanchard Jerrold, *The Life of George Cruikshank.*

88 *early forties.* Vizetelly, *Glances Back,* p. 107.

88 *up a lamp-post!'* W. H. Wills to Blanchard Jerrold, quoted in Jerrold's *Life of George Cruikshank,* 2nd ed., ch. 13.

88 *certainly not home.'* Dickens to Longfellow, Dec 1842 (MS., Princeton University Library).

89 *down Durham Yard.'* G. S. Sala, in *Gentleman's Magazine,* May 1878.

89 *used to recount.* Dickens, quoted in Jerrold, *Life,* vol. II, p. 49.

90 *on the community.* Punch, vol. XIII, p. 92.

91 *ringing voice, FIRE!'* E. and G. Dalziel, *The Brothers Dalziel,* p. 48.

CHAPTER 7. NIL DESPERANDUM

93 *Scollier to him.* John Scollier to Cruikshank, Dec 1847 (University of Virginia Library).

94 *sequel to The Bottle.* George Cruikshank to Anon., n.d. (C. C. Kohler, 'Catalogue of George Cruikshank Sale').

94 *pounds a year.'* G. S. Sala, in *Gentleman's Magazine,* 1878.

94 *temperance speeches.* Quoted in Blanchard Jerrold, *The Life of George Cruikshank,* 2nd ed., p. 241.

94 *Finsbury Bank.* cf. Cruikshank to Cunningham, Feb 1843 (British Library, Department of Manuscripts).

94 *still fight on.'* Kohler, 'Catalogue', ref. 44, *c.*1858.

95 *oblige her.'* Cruikshank to Alfred Crowquill, Sept 1848 (Huntington Library).

95 *come and see her.'* Cruikshank to George Pulford, Jan 1849 (Huntington Library).

95 *back of yours truly.* Cruikshank to Alfred Crowquill, Jan 1849 (Huntington Library).

95 *down at Hythe.* cf. Frederic Stephens, *A Memoir of George Cruikshank,* p. 13.

95 *supper tables.'* W. H. Wills, quoted in Jerrold, *Life,* 2nd ed., pp. 222–3.

96 *for her wages.* cf. assorted receipts in Cruikshank Collection, Middlesex Records Office.

96 *an understated one.'* Hamilton to Bates, quoted in David Borowitz, 'George Cruikshank – Mirror of an Age', paper to William Andrews Clark Library Seminar, 1970, p. 89.

97 *strike a blow.'* George Hodder, *Memories of My Time,* p. 104.

98 *water-drinking.'* Temple Bar (1878), pp. 499 ff.

98 *to stand there.'* Dickens to Cruikshank, 1848 (Gimbel Collection, Yale University).

99 *of your distrust.'* Dickens to
    Cruikshank, April 1851 (Gimbel
    Collection, Yale University).
100 *use of children.* Cruikshank to Anon.,
    Jan 1856 (Kohler, 'Catalogue').
104 *Grand Historical.* E. and G. Dalziel, *The
    Brothers Dalziel*, p. 46.
104 *I shall dash on. . . .'* Cruikshank to
    George Pulford, April 1854
    (Huntington Library).
105 *to all parties.'* Cruikshank to Henry
    Layard, M.P., Feb 1857 (British
    Library, Department of Manuscripts).
106 *to accord me.* John Daniell to
    Cruikshank, Sept 1870, Middlesex
    Records Office (534/14a).

CHAPTER 8. MEMORIALS

107 *at least are innocent.'* Hamilton to Bates,
    1878, quoted in David Borowitz,
    'George Cruikshank – Mirror of an
    Age', paper to William Andrews
    Clark Library Seminar, 1970, p. 88.
108 *bear that process.'* Ibid.
109 *to do ultimately.'* Draft of speech, n.d.,
    Middlesex Records Office.
109 *candlestick-makers.'* Undated draft
    (C. C. Kohler, 'Catalogue of George
    Cruikshank Sale', ref. 72).
110 *against myself.'* Cruikshank to Marquis
    of Salisbury, Feb 1863, Middlesex

Records Office.
110 *upon this earth.'* E. Hurley to
    Cruikshank, Aug 1868, Middlesex
    Records Office.
111 *informing you.'* Duke of Wellington to
    Cruikshank, Aug 1868, Middlesex
    Records Office.
111 *Honorary Colonel.* Ibid.
111 *spirits he has.* G. S. Sala, in *Gentleman's
    Magazine*, 1878.
112 *avowed motto.* Undated draft, Middlesex
    Records Office.
113 *Her Majesty's mind.* George Cruikshank
    to Sir Charles Phipps, undated draft,
    Middlesex Records Office.
114 *upon its travels.'* Cruikshank to National
    Temperance League, n.d. (Kohler,
    'Catalogue', ref. 3 iv).
114 *early as possible.'* J. Taylor to
    Cruikshank, Oct 1866, Middlesex
    Records Office.
116 *by your Lordship.'* Cruikshank to Lord
    Derby, Aug 1867, Middlesex Records
    Office.
118 *treasurer of the fund.* Cruikshank to
    Bruce Committee, undated draft,
    Middlesex Records Office.
118 *the Memorial on.'* Duke of Argyll to
    Cabinet Office, Dec 1873 (British
    Library, Department of Manuscripts).
119 *works of philanthropy.* Printed Memorial
    from Grampian Club, 1873 (British
    Library, Department of Manuscripts).

Bibliography

UNPUBLISHED SOURCES

Beinecke Library, Yale University
British Library: Department of
  Manuscripts; Department of Prints and
  Drawings
Free Library of Philadelphia
Historical Society of Pennsylvania
Houghton Library, Harvard University
  (Widener Collection)
Huntington Library, San Marino, California
The London Library
Middlesex Records Office, London
New York Public Library (Arents
  Collection)
Office of the Registrar-General, London
Princeton University Library (Meirs
  Collection)
Somerset House, London
Stanford University Library (Special
  Collections)
University of Virginia Library
Victoria and Albert Museum: Department
  of Prints
William Andrews Clark Memorial Library,
  University of California

PUBLISHED SOURCES

Personal Memoirs, Essays, Catalogues

Bates, William, *George Cruikshank, the Artist,
  the Humorist and the Man: A Critico-
  Bibliographic Essay* (1897).

Bursill, John, *George Cruikshank, Artist,
  Humorist and Moralist* (1878).
Cohn, A. M., *Catalogue Raisonné of the Works
  of George Cruikshank* (1924).
Cruikshank, George, *The Artist and the
  Author. A Statement of Facts* (1871).
—, *The Bands in the Park* (1856).
—, *The Betting Book* (1852).
—, *A Discovery Concerning Ghosts* (1863).
—, *Drawings by George Cruikshank*, ed. Sir
  B. W. Richardson (1895).
—, *George Cruikshank's Magazine*
  (January–February 1854).
—, *George Cruikshank's Omnibus* (May
  1841–January 1842).
—, *George Cruikshank's Table Book*
  (January–December 1845).
—, *The Glass and the New Crystal Palace*
  (1853).
—, *A Handbook for Posterity or Recollections of
  Twiddle Twaddle* (1896).
—, *The House that Jack Built* (1853).
—, *A Pop-Gun Fired Off in Defence of the
  British Volunteers of 1803* (1860).
—, *A Slice of Bread and Butter* (1856).
—, *Stop Thief or Hints to Householders* (1851).
Dalziel, E. and G., *The Brothers Dalziel: A
  Record of Fifty Years' Work, 1840–1890*
  (1901).
Dickens, Charles, *The Letters of Charles
  Dickens*, Pilgrim Edition, ed. Madeleine
  House and Graham Storey, 3 vols (1965).
Dobson, Austin, 'George Cruikshank',
  Dictionary of National Biography, vol. XIII.
Douglas, R. J. H., *The Works of George*

Cruikshank Classified and Arranged (1903).

Ellis, S. M., *Ainsworth and His Friends* (1911).

George, Dorothy M., *British Museum Catalogue of Political and Personal Satires*, vols VIII–XI.

Grego, Joseph, *Cruikshank's Water-Colours* (1903).

Hackwood, Fred, *William Hone, His Life and Times* (1912).

Hamilton, Walter, *George Cruikshank, Artist and Humorist* (1878).

Hodder, George, *Memories of My Time* (1870).

Jerrold, Blanchard, *The Life of George Cruikshank*, 2 vols (1882).

Kohler, C. C., 'Catalogue of George Cruikshank Sale' (1974) (manuscript in Victoria and Albert Museum).

Krumbhaar, E. B., *Isaac Cruikshank* (1966).

Layard, George Somes, *George Cruikshank's Portraits of Himself* (1897).

Marchmont, F., *The Three Cruikshanks* (1897).

Reid, G. W., *Descriptive Catalogue of the Works of George Cruikshank* (1871).

Stephens, Frederic, *A Memoir of George Cruikshank* (1891).

Thackeray, William Makepeace, 'Essay on the Genius of George Cruikshank', *Westminster Review*, August 1840.

—, *Letters and Private Papers of W. M. Thackeray*, ed. Gordon N. Ray, 4 vols (1945).

Vizetelly, Henry, *Glances Back through Seventy Years*, 2 vols (1893).

Articles, Critical Works

Ashbee, H. S., 'Memoirs of George Cruikshank', *Notes and Queries*, 5th series, vol. 9, 9 Feb 1878.

Bede, Cuthbert, 'Memoirs of George Cruikshank', *Notes and Queries*, 5th series, vol. 9, April 1878.

Cohen, Jane, 'All-of-a-Twist', *Harvard Library Bulletin* (1969).

F., Jas. H., 'George Cruikshank', *Biographical Magazine*, vol. III, 1852.

Feaver, William, *Catalogue of Exhibition of Works of George Cruikshank, Victoria and Albert Museum*.

'George Cruikshank: A Re-Appraisal', ed. Robert L. Patten, *Princeton University Library Chronicle*, vol. XXXV (1973–4). Includes: R. A. Vogler, 'Cruikshank and Dickens'; Louis James, 'An Artist in Time'; David Kunzle, 'Cruikshank's Strike for Independence'; Harry Stone, 'Dickens, Cruikshank and Fairy Tales'.

Harvey, John, *Victorian Novelists and Their Illustrators* (1970).

Kitton, F. G., *Dickens and His Illustrators* (1899).

Layard, George Somes, *Suppressed Plates* (1907).

Lockhart, J. G., 'George Cruikshank', *Blackwood's Edinburgh Magazine*, July 1823.

MacLean, Ruari, *George Cruikshank, His Life and Work as a Book Illustrator* (1948).

Miller, J. Hillis and Borowitz, David, *Charles Dickens and George Cruikshank* (Berkeley, Calif., 1971).

'Portrait of George Cruikshank and Biography', *Fraser's Magazine*, Aug 1833.

Sala, George Augustus, 'Life Memory of George Cruikshank', *Gentleman's Magazine*, 1878.

Sitwell, Sacheverell, *Narrative Pictures* (1937).

Tegg, William, 'Memoirs of George Cruikshank', *Notes and Queries*, 5th series, vol. 9, 15 June 1878.

Thornber, H., 'The Early Works of George Cruikshank', *Manchester Quarterly*, July 1887.

Vogler, R. A., 'Cruikshank's Pictorial Prototypes', *Dickens Studies Annual* (1972).

Wedmore, Frederick, 'Cruikshank', *Temple Bar*, vol. LII, 1878.

Index